Start Your Own
CONSTRUCTION AND LAND DEVELOPMENT
Business

Start Your Own
CONSTRUCTION AND LAND DEVELOPMENT
Business

Adam Starchild

NELSON-HALL nh CHICAGO

Library of Congress Cataloging in Publication Data

Starchild, Adam.
    Start your own construction and land development
business.

    Includes index.
        1. Construction industry—Management.   2. Real
estate development.   3. New business enterprises.
4. Entrepreneur.   I. Title.
HD9715.A2S72   1983   690'.068   83–2366
ISBN 0–8304–1013–9

Manufactured in the United States of America

10   9   8   7   6   5   4   3   2   1

The paper in this book is pH neutral (acid free).

CONTENTS

Making the Decision

If you've reached a point in life where you're tired of working for the other person, and you believe you can make it on your own in a business that you love, join the crowd—you're participating in the Great American Dream of wanting your own business. You know that when you put in a day's work, you earn enough money for your boss to pay your wages *plus* a profit, and you're thinking, Why not have that profit for *yourself*? You believe, and rightly so, that owning and operating your particular kind of business is a worthy aspiration. But do you really know if you are both intellectually and emotionally ready for the demands that owning and managing your own business will make on you?

Perhaps the first thing you should understand is that just being a carpenter (or whatever your building specialty is) doesn't necessarily qualify you for the *business* of building. Even the fact that you're trained in many phases of building won't necessarily prepare you for the myriad of details of managing your own business. On the other hand, the fact that you are competent at your work probably means that you've had to pay close attention to details, from the planning of a complex building job to its completion. The concentration and persistence that you've thus developed are indeed a prerequisite to making a success in your own business.

Some of your initial decisions concerning your new business are basically tactical, and the way you make these decisions depends to a large extent upon how big and complex you expect your business to ultimately become. Your particular idea of the ideal business might be any one of the following: (1) the modernization, remodeling and repair of existing buildings; (2) the construction of buildings for people who have their own building lots, and who supply the design and specifications of the building (this is called custom building, of course); or (3) the construction of buildings on your own lots, on a speculative basis.

What is more likely is that your idea of the ideal business would be a combination of all three of the above. With such a format, you could take advantage of any and all opportunities that might come along, thereby putting yourself in a position to cope with the economic ups and downs of your area. But, like most people, you may have to compromise between what you want, initially, and what you can have. Much will depend upon how much capital you can raise initially. If it's not much, you'll start in remodeling and repair, where your capital investment will be the least, and where the turnover of money will be quickest. If you are a success in remodeling and repair—that is, if your capital grows—you'll undoubtedly want to expand into custom building, which takes considerably less capital than speculative building and returns money relatively faster. Finally, combining these two types of operations with speculative building might be your ultimate goal.

YOUR DAY AS THE OWNER-MANAGER OF A BUILDING BUSINESS

Assuming that you are intellectually ready for the rigors of operating your own building business, are you emotionally ready for the frustrations that you'll probably encounter in this new way of life? Let's return for a moment to our statement, "You know that when you put in a day's work, you earn enough money for your boss to pay your wages *plus* a profit. . . ." You know, for example, that with a good helper you can set roof trusses on a 1,700-square-foot house, and sheath the roof, in two full working days. You know that to do this, you and your helper must work steadily from 8:00 A.M. until 5:00 P.M., with two coffee breaks and a lunch break. This is routine work, in which you can foresee all the contingencies; if the roof trusses don't align properly, you know immediately how to make adjustments and go on with the job, with very little loss of time. You and your helper work well together, and you have systematized the laying and nailing of the sheathing to a point where you know exactly how much you can accomplish in a given time. When you have completed this roof job, you can look at it with a sense of accomplishment— it's a job well done, and done quickly enough that you've earned your wages and earned your boss a profit. But let's look at another kind of day:

As the owner-manager of your own business, you'll probably start your day, along about 7:00 A.M., with a quick look at your local morning newspaper. You do this with the uneasy feeling that it's a waste of time, because you should be out in the Bel-Aire development to make sure that the new man you hired has roughed in a partition, so the plumber won't be held up. But (1) you want to see who has received local building permits, to build what (a swimming pool permit, for example, might call for a fence construction job), and (2) you want to learn the results of the last meeting of the zoning commission regarding the letting of permits outside the city, where they are presently having trouble with the drainage from septic systems.

Next you get in your car and drive out to the Bel-Aire development, where you learn that, not only is your man waiting on the arrival of the plumber, he is also waiting on material that should have been delivered yesterday evening at quitting time but hasn't arrived yet. Your most pressing problem right now is to switch your new man to a different job site while waiting for the plumber to come. By this time, your assistant should be in the office.

At the office, you learn that Mrs. Johnson on Fern Street has called and wants an estimate on the cost of repairing a porch. You give your assistant some instructions which you hope will lighten your workload and drive out to Mrs. Johnson's house. An estimate on a job like this one is difficult because the house is old, and it would take two or three hours' work to determine the condition of the porch foundation. The matter is further complicated by the fact that Mrs. Johnson is old and obviously on a fixed income. If you hold the bid down to meet what you believe to be Mrs. Johnson's financial circumstances, you might lose money. If you hold the bid high enough to meet the demands of any complication, you might lose the job. You make the bid, and Mrs. Johnson says she'll have to think it over and call you back.

By this time it's 10:00 A.M., and you have a 10:30 appointment with your lawyer to go over the details of a contract on some land that you're buying. Since the lawyer is late for the appointment, by the time you've gone over the contract with him, it's lunchtime, and he invites you out to lunch. You accept with the mixed feeling that, while you should be on your way back to the Bel-Aire job, your lawyer is an *important contact* who might be able to help you land a commercial contract.

By 2:00 A.M., you arrive back at the Bel-Aire site, only to learn that the material has arrived but the plumber hasn't. If he doesn't show up today, you'll have to either "make work" for your man tomorrow or send him home—hard choices.

You drive back to your office and call the plumber's shop to learn that he *might* be able to get a man on your job late this afternoon. Now you look over the specifications on the electrical subcontract for one of your jobs. Due to interruptions, you don't finish this until 4:00 P.M. You drive to the Bel-Aire site again; the plumber has arrived, so you have to contact your new man to have him back on the original job in the morning.

You check another job and arrive home at 6:00 P.M. Your wife reminds you of a 7:00 P.M. appointment with a couple to talk about a house that they are planning to have built on their own lot. You keep the appointment, but two hours later the couple is still indecisive—they want time to think it over.

By this time you've been on the job thirteen hours, and your only *tangible* accomplishments are to read over the contract with the lawyer and study the electrical specs—about two hours' work in all. Now your wife reminds you of a social engagement that should be kept.

For a person used to seeing tangible results of efforts, this could be a frustrating and discouraging day, and a tiring one, because of the mental stress. Such frustration is an emotional factor that can cause many persons trouble in making the transition from working for someone to managing their own businesses. However, if you feel that you're emotionally equipped for many of these kinds of days, the satisfactions to be reaped from managing your own business can easily outweigh the frustrations.

SPECULATIVE BUILDING

In your hypothetical day as an owner-manager of your own building business, you were involved in all three of the forms that a building business can take: speculative building, custom building, and remodeling and repair. Assuming that the Bel-Aire development is a group of houses being built for middle-income people, on land that you have bought and developed yourself, this is indeed a speculative project.

On this Bel-Aire project, you have made many initial decisions. After acquiring the land, you decided how many houses to build; chose the architectural design, floor plan, and floor space of each; and selected certain structural details that you hoped would set your houses apart from others in terms of quality. You did all this despite the fact that none of the houses was contracted for. But you did it within the framework of certain knowledge about the economic conditions and housing demand in the area. Moreover, the formidable job of selling the houses is still to be faced. A decision yet to be made is: Will you sell the houses yourself or turn the job of selling over to an experienced realtor?

Your Bel-Aire development has many advantages over both custom building and remodeling—as well as a few disadvantages. One advantage is the complete control that you can exercise over a project of this kind; with no customer "second guessing" you on construction details or bristling with impatience to move in, you can manage the details of each house to the utmost production-schedule advantage. When a house is complete and ready to show, prospective customers can see exactly what they will get if they buy.

One of the most obvious disadvantages of speculative building is the relatively large investment that you will need to get started. Land market prices are increasing in every area of the United States. The availability of water in certain areas is becoming problematic as a result of ever-increasing demand. Sewage disposal is also becoming a problem in areas that are overpopulated because of certain other desirable features. Finally, if you judged the housing market condition incorrectly, or if the economic conditions of your area changed drastically (for example, if a political decision in Washington, D. C., adversely affected the major industry of your area), you may be faced with a delay in selling your houses.

CUSTOM BUILDING

When you talked to the young couple about their plans to have a house built on their own lot, you were acting in your capacity as a custom builder. Custom building sounds like a safe way to conduct a building business, but it too has disadvantages to go along with the advantages. One disadvantage is that, when the typical customer contracts with you to have a house built, he or she immediately becomes an "expert" in all phases of construction and tends to look upon you as a hireling. From a purely professional viewpoint, the customer's judgment is almost always poor, and the demands are unreasonable. Customers can, of course, justify their attitude because the acquisition of a *new home*, with all the emotional connotations that those words convey, is undoubtedly one of the most important events in their lives.

One of the major advantages of custom building is that getting such commercial contracts such as parking garages or shopping centers can considerably increase your earnings. Another advantage of custom building over speculative building is that you can often work on your customer's money. However, your duties as a custom builder do not begin and end with the building of the customer's project. You will probably have to help with the early stages of planning on such matters as building permits, architectural design—and maybe even the acquisition of a lot. Even though such work is not strictly in the realm of the builder, these services are "sales tools." Finally, you will give the customer the contract price on the entire job.

REPAIR AND REMODELING OF EXISTING BUILDINGS

Your estimate to Mrs. Johnson on Fern Street is a part of the remodeling and repair aspect of your business. The major disadvantage of remodeling and repair is that many of the jobs that you land will be small ones. Moreover, these small jobs require about the same amount of planning, time for estimating, adherence to zoning and building codes, and so on that a larger job may take. Many remodeling projects require working under old, existing floors or in attics, or the removal of old partitions, all of which can be dirty jobs. It's not easy to schedule a great many small contracts with much satisfaction to both you and your customers; and the petty annoyances of dealing with the likes and dislikes of many customers will come to the surface more often.

Nevertheless, the repair/remodeling jobs, whether large or small, offer several important advantages, not the least of which is the relatively small capital investment required to take them on. Another advantage is that no other phase of the building business offers as much financial opportunity to the skilled, experienced builder. The building of a house from the ground up has become so routinized that competition forces extremely competitive pricing, but an expertly planned and executed remodeling job can bring you a relatively large margin of profit.

If your first activities in the building business are repair and remodeling, you will have an excellent opportunity to build a reputation for professionalism, honesty, and reliability—important assets in any business. You will be able to develop your management skills and to make contacts that will help you as you expand into speculative and custom building.

And now, a word of caution: While you're building a reputation for honesty, there will be "fast-buck" operators working diligently, not only to undercut that reputation, but to take jobs from you. Almost any householder can tell you about the "contractor" who bid a job on the basis of top-grade material but used poor material on the actual job. Or about the door-to-door roofing contractor who quickly "measured" a 75-square roof to take 100 squares of roofing. The 100 squares of roofing were delivered to the job and distributed around the house for the customer to see; however, as the job was in progress, the contractor hauled away the unneeded 25 squares of roofing.

Your job is to protect your customers from these kinds of shady deals while at the same time building a reputation for honesty for yourself.

A MYRIAD OF DETAILS

As we pointed out earlier, there are a myriad of details to take care of in *any* business, and especially in the building business.

Sales

As a speculative builder, you'll have to decide whether to handle the details of selling houses yourself or use a real estate agency. The agency will take a percentage of the sale as its fee, but on the other hand, the agent considers his or her job a specialty, just as you consider your job a specialty. But perhaps by the time you've progressed this far into building, you'll be as saleswise as any real estate agent. The decision to sell or not to sell can be made later.

In this context the word *sales* refers to selling a finished house. But in another sense, if you are to be successful you must be sales oriented at all times; you must "sell" your reputation, your personality, your experience, your patience, your ability to see a job through. You may do this kind of selling through direct customer contact or through civic activities; whatever your method, this is the kind of selling that will make you prosper in the custom building and remodeling phases of your business.

Acquiring Land

You will undoubtedly find that the acquisition of land is extremely important in speculative building. As we have already pointed out, the day of cheap land is gone in most areas of the United States. Land that once was considered undesirable because it was far from shopping centers or other attractions is often sought out now because it offers the illusion of seclusion or exclusivity. Contradictorily, the prices of city lots are inflated unrealistically, often through the magic of commercial zoning. Moreover, much of the land that you are able to buy will probably be undeveloped—i.e., without streets or utilities. This will add considerably to your cost—to say nothing of the trouble—of starting a housing development. Buying and developing land is a business in itself. But it is a business that you may ultimately have to learn if you are to have enough land to build continuously.

Prefabs and Components

You will have to decide how extensively you will use factory-built components such as prebuilt fireplaces, plumbing systems, or cabinets. Undoubtedly, where the local building codes allow them, these components save time—and time is money. Prefabricated house sections, such as roof trusses, perhaps built in and shipped from Oregon, may be available to you in Indiana. House "packages," consisting of precut lumber, complete with instructions for assembling, are available. Just how extensively you use the factory components, prefabs, and precuts will determine to a large extent how much equipment and how many employees you maintain. And you will soon come to realize that your own opinions of components and prefabs are not the only ones that matter. From time to time, in various localities, components and prefabs have fallen into disfavor with the buying public. Or your decision to use prefabricated plumbing systems (for example) may be offensive to your local businesses, thereby costing you more in the form of future business than it saves you in money.

Subcontracting

You'll know from the beginning, of course, that the letting of subcontracts will be an inherent part of your business. Scarcely any builder—and particularly the small builder—has the skills and equipment to install the electrical system, the plumbing system, and the masonry (to name a few) on a job. Generally speaking, the availability of subcontractors is a decided advantage to you because through subcontracting you will be able to use the skills of licensed professionals who have access, not only to experienced help, but to supplies as well. When you are first starting in the business, the subcontractor can be of tremendous help to you.

Financing for the Customer

No matter which phase of the construction business you are in, the problem of customer financing will arise. Your familiarity with the different sources of housing loans will often make the difference between making or losing a sale, whether it is the sale of a new house or of a remodeling job. Helping your customer arrange financing will be a part of your job as a builder.

LAWS AND REGULATIONS

Thus far I have attempted to point out some of the advantages—and many of the disadvantages—of being in the building business for yourself. Your responsibilities as a builder will be almost endless. Among these responsibilities are:

1. Obtaining permits and licenses.
2. Awareness and understanding of zoning regulations. These may be city, county, or state regulations, including such concepts as land use, river and/or ocean frontage rights of homeowners, and the requirements of commercial zoning in town. In many instances, state regulations concerning septic systems may run counter to county regulations, and it will be your job to understand where the ultimate jurisdiction lies, and how it is applied, if and when disputes arise. You may find that it is advantageous for you to be a member of a zoning commission, and you may find yourself at times embroiled in controversy with the board of county commissioners.
3. Understanding of and adherence to labor laws, both state and federal. Your financial responsibilities to your employees include withholding and paying their state and federal withholding taxes

and FICA taxes. In most states you will be responsible for paying into funds for the employees' unemployment—when and if it should occur—and into compensation funds in the case of employee injury. From a legal viewpoint, these are not matters to be taken lightly, and your accounts will be subject to auditing.

4. Understanding of state and federal income tax laws as they apply to you as a recipient of business income. Now, there is no employer to withhold taxes from your check; this responsibility will fall to you in the form of a *quarterly tax return*, complete with a payment of the *estimated tax*.

LABOR RELATIONS

Understanding labor relations that are *not* regulated by law is also important. For example, if the carpenters of your area are strongly unionized, you will have to decide whether to hire your carpenters through the union or outside it. You will have to decide how many permanent, full-time employees to maintain and what wages they will be paid.

SUMMARY

If all this sounds like it requires too much planning, too much thinking, too much attention to details, too much responsibility, you may decide that owning and operating a building business is not for you. Perhaps I have covered too many of the frustrations and disadvantages, and too few of the advantages and satisfactions—both short term and long term—that you stand to enjoy in your own building business. One of your first satisfactions will be in meeting new challenges and conquering them. Another, as you grow in and with your business, is a new sense of worth and prestige in your community. If your business prospers through your good management, you will prosper financially; you'll be seeking tax shelters in the form of trust funds and retirement annuities and taking month-long vacations. And finally, there is the one advantage that, for most of us, outweighs all the disadvantages: you will have the satisfaction of being the master of your own destiny.

So, if you have concluded that all the duties and responsibilities only serve to make a business of your own more challenging and interesting, you are thinking seriously of trying it. In chapters 2, 3, and 4, I will discuss how to launch and build your business. Chapters 5 through 8 deal with managing the business once it is established. In chapter 9, I will describe actual failures and successes in the building business and analyze why they occurred. In chapters 10, 11, and 12, I discuss ways to make your business grow and how to establish yourself in land development.

2

Considering the Risks

Your attitude, more than your chronological age, is the important factor in your success in business. Age gives experience, maturity, and good judgment; youth gives you aggressiveness, assertiveness, energy, and willingness to take calculated risks. At any age, experience—in either the building trades or some related field—will be helpful. A high degree of interest in building, whether or not accompanied by experience, would seem to be a prerequisite. Perhaps more important than experience or technical knowledge is a *business sense*; with it you may be able to team up with someone who can furnish experience and technical knowledge.

It is the nature of almost any business, and especially the building business, that the owner-operator must assume a responsible position in the community. The more you can participate in community affairs and civic activities, thereby making yourself known to the business community and the general public, the better are your chances of making important contacts that will help you to succeed in business.

RECOGNIZING THE RISKS

We have all seen businesses lining Main Street and in the peripheral sprawl of shopping centers that seem to thrive no matter what the external conditions of weather or economics. We understand, of course, that some of the businesses are subsidized by corporations, but we know that many of them are owned and operated by local businesspersons (such as yourself) and that they must operate at a profit. These businesses have one unique characteristic in common: Except for seasonal sales, they never seem to boom—and they never seem to bust. Not so with the building business.

Economic Conditions

Your business will be influenced by factors that are not under your direct or complete control. For example, the controlling of the prime interest rate by the federal government is an important factor in the construction of new homes in the United States. Oregon, one of the large lumber-producing states, is considering regulations regarding the exporting of logs to foreign countries; this legislation, if passed, will affect the price of lumber and plywood—one way or the other—and will ultimately affect the building industry of the entire nation. The current controversy over the expansion of state parks in the timber-producing areas of the United States may have an outcome that influences lumber prices. When such changes occur, there are usually some rather drastic reactions from the financial community, which will in turn affect the building industry, either for good or bad.

Local conditions will also influence commercial and residential building within a certain area. The acquisition of a new industry—or the loss of one—can change the face of the building business in a given area dramatically.

Such changing economic conditions can cause boom or bust conditions in building. While there would seem to be little that you can do to influence these changing factors, you must at least keep yourself informed of them and try to plan your own activities accordingly. You can, for example, keep yourself posted on regional economic trends by reading the business section of your metropolitan newspaper. You can keep yourself aware of sources of housing loans (such as the FHA) and stay in touch with your local lending institutions; a friendly, knowledgeable banker may be able to inform you of financial trends that will help you in making business decisions.

The Weather

Even in a business boom, prolonged rains or freezing weather can delay building starts while your general overhead expenses continue. But there are ways to combat unfavorable weather. For example, one builder of quality homes keeps a supply of birch plywood stored in his shop, so that in inclement weather his men can build kitchen cabinets that can be quickly installed in the speculative houses that he plans to build as soon as the weather will allow. Another won't hesitate to pour concrete slabs or foundations or do masonry work between heavy rains, because he knows that the rains slow the curing, thereby improving the quality of masonry.

Personal Financial Management

We have already talked about business risks inherent to the building business over which you have little direct control. A general business risk over which you do have control, however, is the management of your personal and family finances. Your ultimate success or failure in business may depend not so much upon earning enough to pay your living expenses as on learning to live on what you can earn—especially in the beginning, when the going is always rougher than later on.

This concept of personal and family financial management can be likened to the problems of a farmer who must supply his farm's water needs from a stream. If he simply installs a pump in the stream, both his water supply and the head pressure will be subject to all the vagaries of the water level in the stream. If, on the other hand, he installs a pump in the stream and *a reservoir above the stream,* into which he can pump water during the flooding season, he will be able to maintain a supply of water as well as a steady head pressure when the stream is low. Applied to personal and family financing, this "steady-head theory" means that you budget your financial needs exactly the same when business is booming as when it is slack; moreover, you should put all income, in excess of short-term budgetary needs, in a savings account (the "reservoir") where it will accrue interest.

Mistakes in Judgment

One manufacturer has said that acquiring the technology to produce an item is often not as complex and problematic as creating or finding a market for the item once it is produced. We have already discussed the way in which changing economic conditions can affect the housing market, often in a surprisingly short time. Judging your market correctly is important.

The Speculative Builder. To succeed as a speculative builder, it is crucial that you work into the proper housing market *in your area*. The worst forms of bad market judgment are: (1) overestimating the size of the market; (2) building houses of the wrong price class; and (3) building houses in undesirable areas.

Before you invest large amounts of money in land and material, you must carefully analyze your area's housing needs. If your area is complex and hard to size up, you should talk to experts, such as real estate agents and bankers, before beginning your project.

The price of homes has been driven up dramatically in the past decade. At first glance this would seem to be of little significance, so long as personal income has risen in the same proportion. But there are other factors to consider; for example, certain segments of the population have been conditioned to believe that they can afford what we casually refer to as middle-income housing—until they try to arrange the financing for their hoped-for new home. On the other hand, an area that would seem to be appropriately classed as "low income" might in fact be in a position to receive an influx of middle-income retirees.

The desirability of certain areas as places to live is subject to change. For example, fairly recently it became "trendy" in certain areas of several Western states to live as far from town as practically possible, without sidewalks or paved streets; this "rustic" living had its appeal—no matter that one, two, or three family members drove their separate cars long distances to and from work and school each day. A shortage or restriction of gasoline may reverse that trend. For the speculative builder, the matter of acquiring land must be judged from the viewpoint of possible future trends as well as trends of the past.

Misjudging the market is not always fatal. With adequate capital, the speculative builder may be able to hold houses until market conditions improve or trends reverse themselves. However, the speculative builder who must continue to make principal and interest payments while the houses stand empty may be forced to let the bank take them.

The Custom Builder. The custom builder's largest

risk is in estimating. In the beginning, you will probably do your own estimating, but as your business grows, you may hire an estimator. Whichever method you use, however, you should always keep a close eye on the estimating because it can make the difference between profit and loss for your company.

The Remodeling and Repair Builder. A grasp of businesslike estimating is perhaps more important in remodeling than in new building. For example, if you bid Mrs. Johnson's porch-repair job with no knowledge of the condition of the foundation, you could in the end lose money on the job. One building contractor has worked out a system of estimating whereby he takes into consideration all the *external* conditions— including the financial (as well as other) circumstances of the customer. For example, he has estimated a roof job approximately 25 percent higher than normal because the customer was facing inclement weather with valuable furniture and personal belongings stored in the unroofed building. To complete the job ahead of the expected onset of rain, he pulled men off other jobs and completed the roof in record time. In the end, he had an appreciative customer. He explained that his overage on that particular job could well be absorbed in a loss resulting from some future miscalculation.

OTHER PITFALLS

Certain pitfalls are common to all three types of builders:

1. Poor supervision of work. Skilled workmen such as you need in the building business demand and get high wages; therefore, they must be kept busy every hour that they are on your payroll. A system of job priorities must be worked out, and workers put first on high-priority jobs. In slack times you should have shop work for those employees that you retain. And most important of all, you should put your most reliable, efficient, and trusted employee in a supervisory position. By keeping workers productively busy, this supervisor will make your company a profit.

2. Poor record keeping. I have talked about the keeping of records for tax purposes, but there is another, no less important, reason for keeping records. A comprehensive system of record keeping should tell you the financial condition of your company at any given time. Detailed material cost records should be maintained, as well as a record of man-hours spent on each phase of each job. When these records are analyzed, they will show where future savings might be made and may even serve as a reference for future estimating.

EVALUATING THE COMPETITION

Most business owners recognize that fair competition creates a healthy business climate. However, if you eventually look around you to see that a competitive speculative builder is selling houses when you're not, or that your competitors in the custom and repair/remodeling business seem to be prospering when you're not, it might be time to ask yourself some questions.

You can be sure that a speculative builder who continually sells houses promptly has judged the housing market of the area correctly. Other factors in such success might be an excellent understanding and use of loan sources, which would provide ample working capital with which to take advantage of opportune land buys.

The stiffer the competition, the more carefully you'll have to bid your custom building jobs. If the competition is such that they underbid you more often than not, you might do well to substitute quality rather than price cutting as an incentive to the customer. Considerable quality in the details of a house can be worked in through craftsmanship. For example, one house builder miters all the corners of the kitchen and bathroom cabinets, which produces an excellent-appearing job and saves the cost of trim.

Competition in the repair/remodeling business might be the stiffest, and it is here, as we have pointed out, that unfair competition might creep in. In such circumstances, expert estimating becomes most important; however, quality work should never be sacrificed to price cutting, because you can build your reputation on quality remodeling jobs.

A DUTY TO SUCCEED

In the early stages of your business, all the responsibilities of management will be on your shoulders. During this time you will establish methods of selling, and you'll soon come to realize that the selling of your reputation is a full-time job. You will establish policies on the maintenance of quality in your work; you will develop procedures for hiring and keeping employees, for analyzing and controlling costs, and for keeping yourself constantly updated on new technology and methods in your field.

Selling

In a manner of speaking, selling is an activity that everyone participates in throughout life—but not always with the intensity of the newcomer to the building business who is determined to succeed. Even if your first venture in the business is in repair/remodeling, you will have to be an aggressive salesperson to keep work up. We have already mentioned the news of building permits as a source of leads, because one remodeling job has a way of creating others. Classified and small display advertising in your local newspaper is often effective (small ads should be run on a sustained basis for maximum effectiveness). Personal contact with businesspeople and others in your own business is important. Establishing a good working relationship with your building supply retailer can work to your benefit. He is in a position to throw considerable work your way.

Establishing a Reputation for Quality Work

When you begin hiring help, you'll know that maintaining quality standards requires teamwork. It is a recognized psychological fact that employees reflect the personality of the employer in matters of "company image," so it is easy enough to instill the quality ethic in your employees.

Hiring Employees

Even though in the beginning you essentially have a one-man operation, you will surely need the services, on a part-time basis, of a bookkeeper, a surveyor, etc., although, strictly speaking, these people won't be your employees. It will be an important day for you and your business when you hire your first full-time, permanent employee; then you will in effect be saying, "My business is now ready to support *two* families instead of *one.*" On the other hand, your first full-time associate might be someone who is willing to form a partnership with you. But in any case, your business now has "another mouth to feed," and both your partner and you should be aware of the profit potential of your business.

Controlling Expenses

The key to controlling expenses is the keeping of complete records. Also, an understanding of what, in the way of equipment and supplies, etc., is essential to your business, and what is not, will curb expenses. For example, renting certain pieces of equipment for occasional use may cost less than buying them. Expenses as they relate to tax exemptions should also be studied, with the help of a tax accountant.

Keeping Up with Technology and New Methods

Construction—as well as all of industry—stands daily on the threshold of new technological, material, and design developments. Some of these new designs may at first meet with customer resistance, while some may be eagerly accepted. You'll keep yourself informed of new ideas in the field of building, and keep abreast of new products that can save you time and money or give you a sales advantage.

YOUR CAPITAL INVESTMENT

Despite your building experience, your enthusiasm, and your determination to succeed, insufficient working capital can cause you to fail in business. Yet, paradoxically, there are cases of men who started in business with limited capital and succeeded. However, there is no denying the need for capital, and their success was at least partially due to working in market conditions in which money was available while their business was in operation.

Where does the money go? There are living expenses, of course. One of the single largest items of expense that you will think about is the acquisition of equipment. Modern and sophisticated equipment, such as backhoe machines, trucks, etc., has a tremendous appeal to the person just beginning in the building business. There are many ways to justify purchases of these items. They are also expensive, and there are many ways to avoid this initial expense.

Items of equipment can be rented, or subcontractors can furnish them along with their services.

Generally speaking, there are three types of companies: the *marginal* company, the *limited* company, and the *growing* company. The classification into which your company falls depends upon the amount of capital you can begin with and maintain.

The Marginal Company

The marginal company operates on minimal capital, thus restricting its activities and profit potential. Just how much it is restricted depends to a large extent upon which building activity the owner hopes to get into.

Speculative Building. Obviously, the speculative-building company is at a bigger disadvantage with minimal capital. It needs more capital than, for example, the custom builder, and considerably more than the repair/remodeling builder. To be anything but a marginal operator—with all the disadvantages the name implies—the speculative building company needs land, and it needs a supply of materials. And even if a builder can find a partner who will supply the land and develop it, he needs capital with which to produce houses when the market demands them. Without the proper market timing that adequate capital can provide, the marginal builder will always be at a disadvantage in the speculative market.

Another disadvantage for the marginal builder who tries to operate in the speculative market is that he generally lacks the equipment that will help him build houses faster, more efficiently, and in the end, more economically. He may ultimately resort to factory components and prefabricated packages, which develop into finished products relatively quickly, thereby turning over capital more quickly.

Custom Building.   Your chances of starting with minimal capital and making it grow are much better in custom building than in speculative building. Since the customer usually provides a developed lot on which to build, and you can often get an advance of money on the contract, you will have more operating capital. If you use this capital judiciously, you may be able to acquire certain items of equipment that will allow you to turn out quality work in a shorter time.

Some experts advise against attempting custom building with minimal capital. They cite as disadvantages the inability to buy equipment that would lower unit costs; this would force you into a precarious bidding position in order to get work. They suggest, as an alternative to conventional building, the use of manufactured houses that can be set up with a minimum of capital and labor.

One builder who began in the custom building business with minimal capital worked this way. When all specifications and plans for a house (or commercial building) on the customer's lot were complete, he would offer a written contract that called for half the asking price in advance. He explained that he needed the money to buy materials. Further, the contract would stipulate that when the work had progressed to a certain point, the customer would pay him the balance of the money owing on the contract. Since this builder had an extremely good reputation for *quality work* and reliability, his method worked well.

Repair/Remodeling. The marginally capitalized company might, with skilled management, work successfully in the repair and remodeling phase of building; however, without skilled management, and without considerable estimating skills, the company would constantly be at a disadvantage. Here, as in custom building, a good strategy is to get an advance of money from the customer. And, as in custom building, your reputation for quality work and reliability will be extremely important to your success.

The Limited Company

I can offer no firm guidelines as to what the word *limited* would indicate to the individual builder, but as a rule of thumb, the company capitalized with limited capital should have a reserve, over and above immediate operating expenses, with which to meet emergencies and/or take advantage of any opportunities that might arise. But this reserve should not be one that is customarily dipped into to meet cost-of-living expenses, regular payrolls, etc.

Speculative Building. As a speculative builder

with limited capital, you might be in a position to buy certain items of equipment that would help you to lower your unit costs, thereby giving you a sales advantage. You might be able to buy land and develop it, maybe even hold it for several months, placing yourself in a better position to gauge the housing market.

Custom Building.   As a custom builder with limited capital, you might be able to stock up on certain standard materials when prices are low. You might be able to buy certain items of equipment that would help you work more efficiently, thereby lowering your total overhead. The very fact that you are not a marginal operator should enhance your position with lending institutions, enabling you to get short-term loans with low-risk interest rates.

Repair/Remodeling.   The major advantage of limited capital over minimal capital in the repair/remodeling business is that you would be able to take on more job starts, thus ensuring yourself of an inflow of cash. Although it is always tempting, it is not advisable to buy items of specialized equipment that might remain in disuse for long periods between those jobs requiring the equipment. Therefore, rent or lease these special items of equipment, and use reserve capital for material with which to start more jobs.

The Growing Company

Again, I cannot offer firm guidelines by which to differentiate between the *limited* and the *growing* company. Generally speaking, the growing company, funded with adequate capital, could survive a short-term economic recession or a slump in local building. It would have enough reserve capital to buy items of equipment when and if needed.

Speculative Building. If you are a speculative builder, adequate capital, together with good long-term financing, will give you many advantages: You will be assured of building sites by options or leases, or through purchases of land. You will be able to buy equipment that will increase your efficiency, save you money in subcontracting costs, or open up new work for you. You can get cash discounts for purchase of material, as well as keep materials on hand as a buffer against ever-rising costs. If you misjudge the housing market, you will be able to hold your houses until they sell, or make adjustments or alterations—such as additional landscaping—that will enable you to sell them. Or you could meet all the financing charges until the houses could be sold.

Custom Building. As a custom builder, adequate capital would allow you to buy certain items of equipment that could save expenses in the form of subcontracting costs, as well as place you in a position to take certain jobs that might otherwise not be available. It would lessen the pressure to bid jobs so low that you would either risk losing money or sacrifice quality on your jobs. You could continue to pay overhead (maybe even keep up the facade of prosperity) during building slumps or recessions.

Repair/Remodeling. Adequate capital would place you in a strong position in the repair and remodeling business. For one thing, it would give you a budget for advertising. For another, you would be able to buy certain items of equipment that would cut your labor costs or allow you to take a bigger variety of jobs. You might even be in a position to offer financing to your customers.

Just how much capital would be considered marginal, limited, or adequate depends upon variables that are unique to each individual situation. The locality, the era, the general U.S. economic outlook, including the unemployment rate and rate of inflation, are all factors in these variables. In the next chapter, we discuss in more detail the amount of capital investment and cash you will probably need.

3

Getting Started in Business

Your method of getting started in the building business will depend to a large extent upon the amount of capital you can raise, and which of the three basic phases of building activities you decide upon. Adequate capitalization for your particular type of business—i.e., speculative building, custom building, or repair/remodeling—as well as some kind of educated projection of the amount of *profit* you might be expected to earn in your first year of business, are the keys to how you will get started in business.

As I pointed out in the previous chapter, it is possible to start in the repair/remodeling business with minimal capital, perhaps even part-time, while you keep your present job. However, I am not an advocate of the part-time business, because it takes enormous energy and a full commitment to make a success of any business, and particularly one that involves as many facets (with their corresponding stresses) as does the building business.

With the technical knowledge that comes from experience, together with some management skills, you might make a successful beginning in custom building with a minimal capital investment. Some of the ways that this might be done were covered in the previous chapter.

If your initial venture is to be in speculative building, you will have to assess your financial situation, as well as your local housing market, accurately. The disadvantages of attempting a beginning in speculative building with minimal capital have been touched upon in the previous chapter. Therefore, your initial questions should be: (1) how much can I earn? and (2) how much capital will I need?

PROFIT POTENTIAL

The word *profit* is often used somewhat ambiguously in different contexts. Moreover, gross profit should be differentiated from net profit. Gross profit is defined as the gross receipts less the immediate cost of production. Applied to the building business, this would mean that the gross profit on a newly built house would be the sale price of the house less the costs of materials and labor, including subcontracting fees. This gross profit would not take into account other expenses, such as a fee for selling the house and the overall costs of acquiring and maintaining equipment, maintaining an office, bookkeeping and/or accounting fees, annual license fees, payroll taxes (such as FICA), and so on.

Net profit, on the other hand, takes into account all these expenses of doing business. However, in the one-man (or small) business, the owners' salaries and income taxes and FICA taxes must still be paid out of the net profit. According to a recent survey, small building contractors made an average net profit of about 14 percent of their gross income in a year.

Whether your projected net profit is 14 percent—or more or less—depends upon your own analysis of the cost factors involved in doing business in your specific area. It also depends upon your opinion of your own managerial ability, because skilled management might raise the percentage figure.

The next step is to protect your expected gross sales for a year. This might be difficult with the repair/remodeling business, but would be less difficult with the custom building business. If your plan is a speculative building project and you are well capitalized, you should be able to project an accurate estimate of your potential earnings. After carefully analyzing all the factors of projected expenses and gross sales—taking into account all the variables—multiply the gross sales figure by the expected percentage figure of net profit. For income tax purposes this will constitute "business income," but you will be able to pay yourself only a portion of this if you are to plow money back into the business for growth and expansion.

How does the net profit percentage figure, multiplied by anticipated gross sales for a year, compare with your present wages? If, after an honest, objective evaluation, it compares favorably, you will want to proceed to the next step in the planning stage, which is the analysis of capitalization. But if the figure is somewhat lower than your present wages, although adequate to meet your family's income needs, you will have to decide if you are willing to trade off income now for the promise of independence and future income potential that a business can give you. If you are willing to make the short-term sacrifice, you will still want to examine the problems of capitalizing a small business.

CAPITALIZATION

The capital needs for a given small business vary from area to area and—more important—from individual to individual. One man may start and operate a marginally capitalized business for many years without apparent personal financial strain or without any desire to expand. Another may begin a marginally capitalized business and begin expanding immediately. Both these cases should be considered exceptions in the business world and not something that you could—or would care to—duplicate. By far the best way to plan the beginning capitalization of a business is through a careful and detailed analysis of your projected operating plan.

The Speculative Builder

As a speculative builder you might be able to begin small, with enough money to build one house (but it is not advisable). From a purely hypothetical view, you could start the house and perhaps borrow on it before it was completed. But this puts you in the position of making mortgage payments until the house is sold.

A more workable financial plan for the speculative builder would be to have the cash to complete one house, ready for sale. When this house is listed for sale you will be in a stronger position in the money market, possibly able to borrow enough on this house to begin another one. Such a procedure would allow you a larger margin of safety, in case the house did not sell immediately, than borrowing money on the partially built house. In any case, an understanding of the housing market would be extremely important, since delayed sales and continuing mortgage payments could be disastrous to your business.

The Custom Builder

How you might get an advance of money from the customer who is providing a lot on which to have a house built was discussed earlier. Some experts frown on this method, saying that the customer resents such a request. The problem, however, is one of customer relations and how much confidence your reputation for honesty and reliability can generate in the customer's mind. Aside from a mutual confidence between you and your customer, the magic ingredient in such an arrangement is in the *written contract*. A typical contract would stipulate that at a certain stage of completion of the house, the customer is to pay you another percentage of the total price. An alternative to this method is to bring the house to a specified state of completion before receiving money from the customer. To implement either plan, you should have a firm understanding with your subcontractors, who will also want to be paid for their work. You will also have to take into consideration the wages of carpenters, helpers, and others that you might employ, which will be due before the completion of the project.

A better plan for the custom builder is to have sufficient capital to complete any job and attendant obligations before receiving payment. With such a plan, you might not be limited to completing one project at a time but could be working on several at once. In such cases, you should investigate the customer's financial responsibility and implement your plan with a written contract with each customer.

Whether you receive money from your customer in advance, before work is begun, when it is in progress, or at completion, the written contract is important, especially for you as a newcomer to the building business. For example, if the customer's construction plans do not include specifications for material grades, types of material, finishing details (does the customer do inside/outside painting, for example, or do you?), these specifications should be ones that you recommend and incorporate into the written contract. It would be well to include in your initial operating expenses a fee for retaining an attorney to help you with the legal intricacies of contracts.

The Repair/Remodeling Builder

Your tangible capitalization in the repair/remodeling business might be the basic equipment (power tools, etc.) with which to work, a credit arrangement with your materials dealers, money to meet other business expenses, such as transportation, wages, and so on, and money to meet your own living expenses until a job is complete and paid for.

Your intangible capitalization would be a knowledge of the repair/remodeling *market:* As a newcomer to the business, how successfully could you compete against already established builders? How often, for example, would your lower bid be rejected in favor of the higher one from a better-known builder? Do you have enough experience in this particular field of building to be sure that your estimates will make the required percentage of profit? Remember, in the beginning you will have no backlog, or overage in bidding, to absorb miscalculations.

I have already touched upon the variety of factors to be considered in figuring capital needs; they are discussed in greater detail in the following sections.

Your Living Expenses

With an average family and average living expenses, your wages as a skilled craftsman in the building trades enable you to maintain a good standard of living. This standard of living is based upon an income of X dollars per week or month. In addition to wages, you may receive fringe benefits in the form of bonuses, paid vacations, and paid hospital and surgical plans for you and your family. If your budget needs are based upon take-home pay, you will probably have an additional income each year in the form of state and federal income tax refunds. If this total annual income is needed to maintain the standard of living that you want, you, as a self-employed business-man, will have to pay yourself this amount—or you will have to make certain unpleasant adjustments in your standard of living.

Good household management might help in trimming or adjusting a home budget to meet the demands of starting a new business; however, good management will not take the place of money in meeting your continuing living expenses. Whatever these needs are, they should be included in your capitalization plans for the new business. The following guideline is also offered, as a rule of thumb. You should have in a savings account at least enough money for six months' living expenses, provided the first six months are in the height of the building season.

Office Expenses

When you are starting out, an office may not seem important. But you will want a telephone business listing, and the appropriate place for such a phone is in whatever you will ultimately designate as your office. Ideally, your office should be large enough, and located in such a manner, that it will serve several purposes: (1) as a place for keeping records; (2) as a place to meet with customers; and (3) as a place to work on plans, specifications, etc. There are several ways of economically acquiring office space:

The Home Office.   The home office has an advantage for income tax purposes, inasmuch as that portion of the total footage of your house can be allocated as an office, provided (under the most recent tax ruling) you use the space exclusively in connection with your business and have no other place to do this business. Therefore, for the purposes of business capitalization, do not look upon the home office as "free space"; a portion of your home utilities and your rent or mortgage payment and interest can be allocated as a business expense.

Mobile Home or Travel Trailer. Another method of acquiring office space is to set a travel trailer or small mobile home on a lot. The total initial cost of such an office would include the cost of the lot. These costs can be determined by checking prices in your area.

Rented Office Space. Your capital investment in rented office space would be determined by the price and terms of the rental. When you have decided which type of office suits your needs and situation best, you will decide if an office is a necessity for doing business in the beginning. If it is, you can compute your capital needs for office expenses on the same basis that you computed your living expenses; that is, assure yourself of enough capital to maintain an office for at least six months while establishing yourself in business.

Incidental expenses to plan for in maintaining an office are:

1. Office equipment. As office equipment, the following items are necessary: A desk, a drafting table, an office copier, a filing cabinet, a typewriter, a ten-key adding machine, a stapler, and miscellaneous office furniture to your own taste. Whether you buy all these items immediately will be your decision to make, but you will eventually consider

them as minimal. Whether you buy the items new or used (or new *and* used) will determine how much cash outlay you need for office equipment. Careful shopping pays off in acquiring equipment and furnishings for the office.

2. Office supplies. Your basic needs for office supplies will be printed forms for contracts, billing forms, and ledger sheets for record keeping. Forms should preferably be imprinted with your company name. Printed letterheads and envelopes for correspondence are helpful, but not a must. Printed business cards are almost a necessity. The cost of business cards, printed letterheads, etc., can be allocated to advertising. The remaining office supplies are small items, such as paper clips, staples, copy paper, etc. The total cash outlay for these items will run from $100 to $150 as a minimum.

3. Business telephone. The cost of a separate telephone for your business can be easily determined by calling the telephone business office of your area. It should include the cost of a business listing in the next directory that will be published.

Tools and Equipment

There is little to be said in a book for the experienced builder regarding the necessity for, and prices of, tools and equipment. By the time you have decided to go into business for yourself, you will probably have acquired many hand and power tools of your own. As for equipment that you were not expected to provide as an employee, such as ladders, scaffolding, house jacks, concrete mixers, masonry saws, etc., these items can be rented or leased in the beginning. Decisions to buy new, sophisticated, and expensive items of equipment should be made wisely and judiciously. Talk to a tax accountant about the various advantages and disadvantages of equipment leasing as opposed to purchasing. Learn the details of the current tax ruling regarding the depreciation of the value of equipment. This factor will enter into the computation of your capital investment in equipment.

Meeting the Payroll and Payroll Expenses

List the labor that you anticipate using, such as carpenters, helpers, brick masons, etc. Allow yourself enough available capital to meet this payroll before receipts start coming in. In a detailed analysis, differentiate between those workers who are your full- or part-time employees, and those who are self-employed contractors (there will be an additional expense incurred for employees in the form of state unemployment taxes). If you plan to use a full- or part-time bookkeeper, secretary, or telephone receptionist, don't forget to include his or her wages in your computations.

Acquiring Land

If you plan to venture into speculative building soon, you'll need additional capital for land. In some cases, land might be available on credit; for example, the owner might take your personal note for lots, to be paid when your completed houses sell. But even so, you will need cash to pay for the incidental expenses of acquiring and developing land, such as title searches, surveying, etc. You should also consider the expenses incurred in the developing of land.

Materials

Your unique situation will determine how much building material you will need in the beginning. There are traditionally two ways of acquiring materials—with cash or credit. Buying on credit might ease the capital needs in the beginning, but there are usually carrying charges in these kinds of purchases, which ultimately increase your operating expenses. The best way to compute capital needs for material is to consider both your short-term and long-term needs.

Short-Term Material Needs. Your most pressing short-term need might be enough to build your first custom or speculative house, or enough material to get you started on the several repair/remodeling jobs that you have lined up. Your immediate capital needs will be determined by (1) the availability of material on credit, and (2) a projected date when you can expect cash receipts from your first completed job, or the sale of your first speculative house.

Long-Term Material Needs. Your long-term material needs will be influenced by (1) discount prices available for quantity buying, (2) your storage facilities, (3) expected price fluctuations. For example, if you know that certain grades of lumber that can be stored outside, such as 2x4 studs or other framing lumber, are soon to have a price rise, you may want to buy quantities of them to have on hand.

Incidental Expenses

If you've ever tried to maintain a home budget, you know that the great wreckers of budgets are those incidental expenses that are neither foreseen nor planned for. A broken appliance, for example, must be repaired; likewise, a broken piece of building equipment must be repaired. Your first legal questions, or surveying needs, will result in fees that you may not have planned for. List everything that you can think of, so you can determine exactly how much capital to allow for them.

Those Miscellaneous Expenses

Another budget wrecker are those ''miscellaneous'' expenses that you *should have* allowed for but didn't. Unexpected social obligations, price rises—all can alter your capital needs once you begin in business. So, in computing the final figure for your capital needs, if you err, do so on the high side. Add as much as 10 percent to your final figure for a safety factor.

OPERATING CASH

In addition to your initial capital investment, you will need operating cash for day-to-day operating expenses. If a reservoir of cash is to give you a continuing cash flow, it should be "filled" in the beginning.

The amount of cash that you'll need will depend upon what you are building and what your mode of operation is regarding material purchases, etc. One way to estimate your cash needs is to design a week-by-week cash schedule on the jobs that you are committed to. You might know, for example, that your first week's expenses will include the costs of permits, plans, earth-moving work, premixed concrete for the foundation, and a charge to get the plumber, a subcontractor, on the job. In the expenses of the second week, there will be some carry-over of the activities of the first week, and additionally, some masonry work by a subcontractor whom you want to pay immediately. By the third week, your payroll is due and must be met, and so on. If this is a custom house, perhaps you know that by the eighth week you will get some cash receipts in the form of a payment from your customer; these receipts will go into your cash reservoir.

The following suggestions for making a schedule of cash flow are offered as a guideline; however, you must actually compile your own schedule depending upon your initial amount of cash and how you plan to handle receipts and disbursements. These factors in turn depend partially upon whether your initial activities are as a custom builder, a speculative builder, or a repair/remodeling builder. Assuming that you want to operate on the smallest possible cash budget in the beginning, here are some suggestions:

The Custom Builder

1. Get an advance of money from the customer. This technique has been described earlier.
2. Work with customers who furnish their own land.
3. Buy materials only as you need them, using maximum credit.
4. Minimize your vehicle costs by asking your suppliers to furnish delivery.
5. Minimize your equipment expenses by renting or leasing equipment whenever possible.
6. Use space in your home for an office.
7. Minimize the expenses of maintaining a payroll by using subcontractors whenever possible.
8. If you can effect a saving by using precut materials or prefabricated houses, use them.
9. Manage your own work duties carefully, allowing time for the supervision and planning of work, eliminating costly delays.

The Speculative Builder

As a speculative builder, you can use all the money-saving steps outlined above and additionally:
1. Do not branch out into related businesses, such as earth-moving, real estate sales, or money lending.
2. Do not handle second mortgages on your houses or sell them on lease options

3. Let your first house be a demonstration house, so that subsequent houses can be built on a custom basis.
4. Find a partner who might furnish land, land development expenses, or direct financial support.
5. Follow all the suggestions in this book for building marketable houses in your area, thereby assuring quick sales.

SOURCES OF CAPITAL

Where does capital come from? Excluding such windfalls as contest awards and unexpected inheritances, it comes from such conventional sources as your savings account, from bank and savings and loan institution loans, from credit that your material suppliers will extend to you, from personal loans, and—if you should decide to incorporate your business—from the sale of stock.

Loans

To the lending institution, money is a commodity, just as 2x4s are a commodity to your lumber dealer. The major difference is, once you have bought the 2x4s, your lumber dealer doesn't really care what you do with them, so long as payment for them is received. Your banker, on the other hand, hopes that you will establish a good performance reputation with the bank's money, because the reputations of the bank's borrowers reflect on the reputation of the bank. When borrowing, ask the loan officer to explain to you the amount of interest and the method of computing it. Then you will be able to calculate exactly how much your money is costing you.

Personal Loans.   Sometimes it is possible to get a loan from a friend or relative without interest charges. The manner in which such a loan is secured is usually a personal matter between you and the lender. He or she might want a personal note for a year or so.

Loans from Personal Finance Companies.   If turned down by a bank, some people are tempted to borrow from a personal finance company. The two major disadvantages of borrowing from a finance company are: (1) the interest rates of finance companies are usually higher than those of banks and savings and loan institutions, and (2) certain state and federal regulations impose limitations on how much money a finance company can loan. If you can't get adequate capital in a loan, you are better off not borrowing, since undercapitalization is a serious failing of many small businesses.

Incorporation

In a later chapter, I will explain in some detail the advantages and disadvantages of the corporation over the single proprietorship or partnership, as well as some guidelines to follow in the forming of a corporation. One factor in the sales of stock of a new corporation is the amount of confidence the corporation can generate in the minds of stockholders. However, a family corporation may be formed if some family member has enough money, property, or equipment to make a meaningful contribution to the capitalization of the corporation.

Credit

In a sense, credit is a substitute for capital, but the long-range effects of credit must be studied carefully. For one thing, does your credit buying force you into a position of having to buy from one dealer? Are the carrying charges that are added to the cost of materials higher than the usual interest rates of lending institutions?

Credit from Subcontractors.   The subcontractor may have an empathy, or understanding, for you, because he may remember the problems of beginning a new business. If he has a good reputation for fairness and honesty, watch closely how he handles the matter of extending credit; from this, you can gain valuable experience.

Credit from Landowners and Developers.   Don't hesitate to work with these persons whose interests are essentially the same as yours. They want you to succeed, because when houses are sold, building sites are also sold.

TYPES OF MORTGAGES

You or your customers will get your building project or home financed through one of the following:

1. The Federal Housing Administration (FHA). The FHA does not lend money directly but guarantees, or insures loans for housing. For example, it insures loans made for the financing of repairs to homes. You can get more detailed information about FHA loans from FHA approved lenders, such as banks and savings and loan associations. You cannot apply directly to the FHA for a loan, but your customer can apply through an FHA approved lender.

2. The Veterans Administration (VA). Nearly all veterans are eligible for loans through the insured loan program of the Veterans Administration. As much as 95 percent of the cost of a home can be financed through the VA loan program, and terms are better than through many other sources. If your customer qualifies for a VA loan, tell him or her that the money is easier to obtain this way than through many other government programs.

3. Local Building and Loan Associations. Any relationship that you can establish with your local building and loan association will be invaluable to you, because this association can help keep you informed about the economic conditions of your area. Moreover, it is traditional for an officer of the association to make an appraisal of a house before approving a loan. His or her approval will enhance your reputation as a quality builder.

4. Banks. When your customers go to the bank for a housing loan, they are bargaining with both their own reputation for financial responsibility and your reputation as a builder of homes that meet certain specifications and standards of quality. Generally speaking, banks will lend only up to a

certain percentage of their appraised market value of a house.

5. Insurance Companies. Certain large insurance companies have been making money available for housing, either through FHA insured loans or directly without FHA insurance.

6. Cooperative Financing Groups. In some communities, local cooperative groups make some type of financing available to its members. Attention to and awareness of your customers' financing is an extremely important part of your building package. Don't tie up your own money in materials and commitments until you are sure that financing is available.

WHAT IS SALABLE?

Before you can complete your figures on how much capital and operating cash you'll need, you'll have to analyze the market to see what types of houses—in what price range—are selling in your area, or in the area where you have planned to build. Social, economic, and geographical factors will determine the style and the price range of the houses that sell in your area.

THE TRANSITION BETWEEN PLANNING AND DOING

By now I've thrown a lot of facts and figures at you and couched them in conservative language because

I'm not promoting "blue sky," but down-to-earth business facts. I have also stressed the concept of *planning*. To certain individuals, planning is a boring process. If you are that type of individual, you most likely will not like the building business when you are in it.

On the other hand, to other types of individuals, planning is an invigorating—even exciting—process. These individuals enjoy planning and then watching the details of the plans take effect. If you are this type of person, you will enjoy the business aspects of building.

Your like or dislike of planning is not the only—and perhaps not the most important—factor in your success in the building business. Various other factors will be discussed in the chapters that follow.

4

The Legalities of Starting a Business

Generally speaking, there are certain procedures that the owner of a new business must go through concerning permits, licenses, the registration of a business name, etc. For example, most communities have laws and ordinances that apply to businesses within the limits of the community. In some instances, a county license or permit may be additionally required for work that a business conducts within the county. And there may be certain state requirements that will have to be met before your business is legal.

City, county, and state laws and ordinances vary greatly across the United States. For example, a city that imposes a city sales tax will probably require the owner of a business within the city to file information regarding the nature of his or her business, for sales tax purposes. Most states require that you register your firm name in the appropriate state office. States that impose a sales tax may want information regarding the nature of a business, how much equipment was purchased (if an already established business is bought), and various information pertaining to the collection, filing, and payment of sales tax. The best way to learn about the laws and ordinances of your particular city, county, and state is to check with the appropriate government offices. Better yet, talk to a local attorney about these requirements.

OWNERSHIP

There are three forms of ownership under which you can organize your business: (1) single proprietorship, (2) partnership, and (3) corporation. Again, to be confident of your legal status under one of these forms of ownership, you should consult an attorney. The following general rules pertaining to various forms of ownerships are offered as a guideline.

The Single Proprietorship

The single proprietorship is obviously the most simple to organize, and it is the one used for many small businesses across the nation. If, for example, you were to assume a business name for your one-man business that is the same as your first name and surname (such as "Joe Smith Builders"), you would probably find the legal intricacies of registering your business name to be quite simple, as compared to registering a company name.

The single proprietorship gives you freedom of operation, limited only by city, county, and state laws governing businesses in general. The most stringent of these laws apply to the keeping of proper records for tax purposes. You should seek the help of a tax accountant, who can advise you on what your responsibilities as a single-proprietor owner will be to meet the various licensing rules mentioned earlier.

Many of the advantages and disadvantages of the single proprietorship are largely subjective. You would probably enjoy the freedom of movement that it gives you, the ability to make spot decisions, and the minimizing of delays in making estimates with no partner or stockholders to be responsible to. On the other hand, you may find taking all the responsibilities and risks to be too much of a burden for a lone individual.

Even if you begin with a single proprietorship, as your business grows you will delegate responsibilities and authority to certain of your employees, in specified areas of the business. And you will undoubtedly see opportunities that could be taken if someone with a vested interest in the business were available with capital, ideas, or the willingness to work. By that time your business will probably be large enough to support a partnership.

The Partnership

A partner that you take into the business, either at the outset or after the business is established, should come in with some assets. Some of these assets may be tangible and some intangible. Among the tangible assets might be additional capital, equipment, tools, or business contacts. Among the intangible assets might be additional skills, enthusiasm, a personable approach to customer relations, and life goals common with your own.

One of the most common causes of the failure of a partnership is personality problems between the partners. The typical syndrome of this failure is somewhat as follows. One partner, the more aggressive of the two, assumes more responsibility and takes on more duties than the other. By these actions the other partner sees himself or herself being relegated to a second-rate or subordinate position in the company, and in reacting compounds the problem by refusing to take even a fair share of responsibilities and duties. The first partner sees this response as laziness, and the personal relationship between the two, which seemed so well founded in the beginning, deteriorates. There would seem to be no cure for this kind of human behavior, but some of the problems inherent in a partnership might be avoided by drawing up a partnership agreement, in the form of a legal document, outlining the duties and responsibilities of each partner in the event that one of them pulls out of the business. This should be done with the help of an attorney.

The major disadvantage of a partnership is the unlimited liability that each partner must assume. This liability is an important consideration in the building business, with its high risks. Partnerships are seldom used in the building business, for this and other reasons.

The Corporation

The corporation, though more complex in its structure than either of the other two forms of ownership, offers some important advantages for the small builder. A major advantage is that the liability of an investor for the debts of a corporation is limited to the amount of his or her investment. As an example of the advantages of limited liability, consider the case of one single-proprietorship, speculative builder. He lost all of his houses because an economic slump stopped sales. The houses were eventually sold in forced sales to satisfy the demands of the mortgage holder and other creditors, but the sale didn't bring in enough money to pay all the debts that the builder had incurred. Through court judgments, the builder was held responsible for all his debts, despite the fact that his main assets—the houses—were gone. If the builder had been operating under the limited disability of a corporation, he probably would have been liable only to the extent of his investment in the corporation.

The corporation also offers certain tax advantages. Considering the risks and complexities of a building business, you may want to consult an attorney concerning the advantages and disadvantages of forming a corporation.

NAMING YOUR FIRM

I pointed out earlier that a single proprietorship business may be carried on under your own name.

While there would seem to be no uniform law across the nation regarding the naming of a single-proprietorship business, such a name would not usually include the word *Company*. If a few simple rules are followed in the naming of a business, there is little or no risk of infringement upon other business names that are registered in state offices. The most current ruling in Oregon (as an example) regarding business names is as follows:

> 648.010 Registration of assumed business name required; application for registration. (1) No person or persons shall carry on, conduct or transact business in this state under any assumed name or under any designation, name or style, other than the real and true name of each person conducting the business or having an interest therein, standing alone or coupled with words which merely describe the business carried on and do not suggest the existence of additional owners, unless such assumed name or designation, name or style has been registered with the Corporation Commissioner. Words which suggest the existence of additional owners within the meaning of this section include such words as 'Company,' '& Company,' '& Sons,' '& Associates' and the like.

The foregoing is only an excerpt of Section 648.010 of the Oregon assumed business name law. In its entirety, the section says in essence that any *assumed* business name must be registered. The registration form must include, among other information, the real and true names of persons conducting the business, the counties within the state in which the firm will conduct business, etc.

Still another section of the law states that if one attempts to register with the corporation commission an assumed business name that is "the same as, or deceptively similar to, an assumed business name already registered for a county designated in the application," the corporation commissioner shall not register the assumed business name.

The above excerpts from Oregon state laws regarding assumed business names are offered only as guidelines, and other states may have laws that differ. What the laws would suggest is that Joe Smith, for example, might name his business Joe Smith Home Building but not, for the sake of style, "Joe Smith Building Company," without falling into the category of an assumed business name with its attendant responsibilities of registration, risk of infringement, etc. As applied to a partnership, Joe Smith and Bob Jones could call their firm "Smith & Jones, Builders," but not "Smith & Jones Building Company," without falling into the category of an assumed name, because the word *Company* implies other owners.

If your state has laws similar to those of Oregon regarding assumed business names, you—or you and your partner—will consider the advantages and disadvantages of the assumed business name. If you decide upon an assumed business name, you may want it to be associated with your particular city, county, area, or region rather than your own name. For example, a business located along a coastal area might be called South Coast Builders, North Coast Builders, or Seaside Builders. (The trouble inherent in names with a local or regional flavor is that it is extremely difficult to use one that is not "the same as, or deceptively similar to, an assumed name already registered.'')

You may want to assume a name that suggests quality, reliability, or honesty, such as Homes of Quality or Reliable Builders. The chances are, such a name will have to be registered in your state. If you decide upon such a name and want to enlarge upon the theme of quality—or whatever—that you have chosen, you may want to accompany it with an emblem, insignia, or company logo. Again, insignias must be designed with care and originality so that you will not infringe upon someone else's design. Such insignia or marks, which are called trademarks, will probably have to be registered in your state.

The considerations for naming a corporation are much the same as those for naming the single proprietorship and partnership business, except that the word *Incorporated* (usually abbreviated *Inc.*) should also be included.

Another legal consideration in choosing a name is that it must not imply a connection with some entity, living or dead, when no such connection in fact exists, or permission has not been granted to use the name in such a manner. For instance, the inclusion of the name ''Frank Lloyd Wright'' into your business name would imply some connection with the late, well-known architect, and if your own name is not also Frank Lloyd Wright, your state commissioner would almost certainly question the legality of your use of the name.

Select your business name carefully. Names serve several purposes besides the functional purpose of identification. Make it a name that you can live with for a long time, because, just as your own name, it will become a part of your personality. If you determine that you must register an assumed name in your state, be sure the name has cleared registration before lettering signs on your office and truck and purchasing printed letterheads.

PERMITS

It is extremely unlikely that you will begin your business in an area where no permits of any type are required to conduct a building business. Inquire at the local city hall concerning city permits; inquire at the county court house of the county in which you operate concerning county permits, and at the county surveyor's office regarding state permits. Be aware, also, that the fact that your business is located and licensed in one county *might not* absolve you from the responsibility of obtaining a permit to do business in an adjacent county.

BUILDING CODES AND ZONING LAWS

Building codes and zoning laws have been around for many years, in one form or other. Although some operators see them as an infringement on personal rights, they are in truth a way to protect the investments of property owners. Whatever your feeling about their purpose and intent, it is your responsibility to understand and adhere to them, because the codes and laws are enforceable.

Building Codes

Check on building codes that might be in effect at the city level, the county level, and the state level. A thorough understanding of the various codes, even as they apply to work done by subcontractors, is essential. If, for example, most of your previous experience has been confined to building within a certain city's limits, you may find that your first job in the county's jurisdiction has more stringent codes for sewage and septic systems. A knowledge of such codes would be vital to you despite the fact that you subcontract the installation of plumbing.

Zoning Laws

As with building codes, zoning laws might vary between adjacent cities in the same county, or county laws might (and usually do) differ from city laws. Further, certain state and/or federal laws might apply in certain areas where you work. Generally speaking, if a city has a city manager system, the city manager can advise you on city zoning laws. The board of county commissioners usually determines and administers county zoning laws. Information on state zoning laws is usually obtainable at the county court house. *It is extremely important that you do not begin a building project without a thorough knowledge of the various zoning laws as they apply to the particular area in which you intend to build.*

EMPLOYER RESPONSIBILITY

In an earlier section I touched on the responsibilities of the employer in withholding, reporting, and paying of the various state and federal withholding taxes, state compensation, and so on. Additionally, there are state laws dealing with child labor, working conditions, and minimum wages. If your work involves interstate commerce or government contracts, there will be federal laws applicable to that phase of your business. It is best that you get information regarding your obligations to employees from your attorney.

Insurance

Like insurance for your family or personal needs, insurance for your business needs can be broadly classified into four types: health, life, casualty, and liability.

Health Insurance. You will probably not be legally obligated to provide health insurance for your employees, but most large businesses, as well as a few small businesses, voluntarily participate in group health insurance plans that include benefits for employees. These benefits are usually provided for employees as fringe benefits, which are in effect an increase in their wages. It is sometimes possible for the very small employer to participate in a group health insurance plan.

Life Insurance. Many businessmen buy the relatively low-cost term life insurance on their own lives, with provisions to make the partner or spouse the beneficiary. This protects the business against failure during the transition time immediately following the untimely death of the principal of the firm. Most business partners buy this kind of life insurance on a reciprocal basis.

Casualty Insurance. Depending upon the terms of a casualty insurance policy, this type of insurance is designed to help you recover losses incurred through accidental damage to your property, vehicles, equipment, etc. Coverage for theft losses is also included in many casualty insurance policies. If you secure financing to buy equipment, the lending institution will probably require that you provide casualty coverage for the equipment being financed.

Liability Insurance. In most states, employers are required by law to carry liability insurance to cover employees in case of accidents on the job. In some states, the state itself sponsors the insurance plan, and the premium is paid as part of the payroll deductions of each employee. Alternatively, in some states the employer is permitted to buy this liability coverage from a private insurance company. Whatever method of securing coverage is used, you will almost certainly find that this particular kind of liability insurance is one of your enforceable obligations as an employer. Even if it is not required by your state, you should provide this employee coverage to protect yourself from expensive lawsuits that might result from employee accidents.

You will probably also want liability insurance to protect you in case of personal or property damage to others as a result of activities of your business. Sufficient insurance coverage in this important area will also protect you from expensive lawsuits, or help pay court judgments if they do arise.

Talk over your insurance needs with an insurance agent. But don't be misled to believe, on the one hand, that maximum amounts of all forms of insurance, with large premium payments, are compulsory; or on the other hand, that you can survive indefinitely in the building business without adequate casualty and liability insurance.

Taxes

I have already mentioned some of the taxes that you as a businessman will be liable for. In many respects, these taxes are dramatically different from those you paid as an individual. Furthermore, it is almost mandatory that you set up a system of tax accounting. Since your time and knowledge will be devoted to the everyday problems of establishing your business, you will benefit from the services of a tax accountant. But even with a tax accountant, certain duties will fall to you (or your bookkeeper); for instance, you will need to set up a system of simple record keeping, and from the very outset, keep all cash tickets and cancelled checks that relate to any type of purchase that you make for your new enterprise. Don't make the mistake in the early stage of your business of thinking that you can keep records in your head until some future time when conditions will be more ideal to set up a system of record keeping. Such details as dates, amounts, etc., are too easily forgotten.

The following are a few of the taxes that you will probably encounter in your business.

Payroll Taxes. Generally speaking, the employee shares the financial burden of payroll taxes with you, but the responsibility for keeping records on each employee, and for periodically reporting and paying his or her applicable taxes, is yours. The typical taxes that are either withheld from the employee's wages or paid by you (or both) are the federal withholding tax, state withholding tax (if applicable in your state), unemployment fund contribution, and the Federal Insurance Contributions Act tax—or FICA, upon which the employee's future social security payments will be based.

Business Income Tax. As either an individual owner or a partner in a business, you are now responsible for withholding, reporting, and paying your own income tax as well as your own FICA tax. To do this correctly and to your own best advantage, you must calculate all the expenses relevant to doing business. These expenses are deducted from the gross income of the business to arrive at a net profit figure, upon which you will be required to pay income taxes. It is impossible to enumerate all the possible business expenses that are allowable as expenses, for tax purposes, against the gross income of a business, but the following are offered as a general guideline:

1. Expenses for labor. These include wages and salaries paid to permanent and part-time employees as well as to subcontractors.

2. The cost of supplies. All materials and supplies that you purchase to be used in your business are a direct expense to offset the gross income of your business. However, generally speaking, any supplies or materials that are not used in the year they are purchased must be carried on an inventory into the following year and charged as an expense in the year in which they are used. Cash tickets from your suppliers, showing the dates and amounts of purchases, are the most acceptable forms of proof for this type of expense.

3. Overhead expenses. At the outset, you must be aware that IRS rulings regarding allowable overhead expenses are subject to changes and revisions from time to time. A general outline of expenses that are currently allowable business expense deductions is as follows.

    a. Depreciation. Generally, tools, equipment, etc., depreciate in value from the time they are purchased. This depreciation (but not the full cost of the item) is considered an annual business expense. While the rules for depreciating equipment, etc., may change, the necessity for keeping records of the dates and amounts of purchases does not change.

    b. Taxes on business and business property, and/ or

    c. Rent on business property.

    d. Repairs.

    e. Insurance.

    f. Legal and professional fees (such as attorney's fees that are directly related to establishing your business, etc.).

    g. Commissions (such as sales commissions paid to agents, etc.).

    h. Amortization. Even as this is written, the current ruling on amortization is being revised, pointing up the need for the services of a tax consultant.

    i. Pension and profit-sharing plans and other employee benefit programs.

    j. Interest on business indebtedness.

    k. Bad debts arising from sales or services.

    l. Depletion.

    m. Business-related travel expenses. At this writing, business-related travel expenses may be computed either on a flat-rate mileage schedule or by keeping complete records of expenditures for such items as gas, oil, and repairs.

    n. The cost of meals and lodging while away from home on business trips, subject to certain exclusions and the most current tax ruling.

The foregoing list of currently allowable business expenses should by no means be taken as complete and authoritative, but it should give you some idea of the extensiveness of the record keeping that is necessary in relation to taxes.

As a business owner, your Form 1040 will now be accompanied upon its return to the IRS with various other forms, such as "Schedule C—Profit (or Loss) from Business or Profession'' and various other forms to substantiate your claim to certain business expense allowances.

As a self-employed person, you are also obligated to pay the full amount of your own FICA taxes, the amount of which is either a percentage of your earnings up to a specified maximum or determined by the most current ruling regarding FICA taxes.

Usually, the IRS requires that you estimate your expected annual net income and make quarterly income tax payments based upon this estimated amount. Then, at the normal time for filing income tax forms and making the annual payment, the quarterly payments are used as a credit to offset your tax obligation.

Not only do you have a tax obligation to the federal government, but also, in most states, you have an obligation to file forms and pay state income taxes. The rulings regarding state income taxes may differ from those regarding federal income taxes, or they may adhere closely to federal rulings, depending upon your state.

Inventory Tax.   Usually, where an inventory tax is applicable, it is administered by a county assessor and made payable to the county where your business is located. In many counties the inventory tax is applicable to items of equipment, as well as supplies, merchandise, etc., that you may have on hand at a specified date in the tax year. If you are obligated to pay an inventory tax, you will have to keep inventory records.

Sales Tax.   Certain states, cities, or counties may have a sales tax. Generally speaking, where a sales tax is in effect, it is applicable to the sales of certain types of merchandise, and the financial burden of the tax is your customer's. However, you have the responsibility for collecting the tax from the customer, keeping records on it, and filing and paying it.

Specific information on federal, state, and local taxes is available from a variety of sources (for example, the telephone numbers and addresses of regional IRS offices are usually included in the booklet that accompanies the tax forms that are sent to you each year). However, you should understand that any information given you by an IRS representative will not keep you out of trouble if your tax records are found not to be in order. In any case, you are better off to turn the complexities of your state and federal income taxes over to a tax accountant. And in special, highly complex cases, you may have to consult with a tax specialist. His or her fee will probably be a deductible item on your next income tax return.

DO IT LEGALLY

Philosophers and common people alike have long debated the morality of taxes and the many laws that apply to businesses, and they have often seen them as infringements upon our personal freedoms. However, you as a businessperson are well advised to understand the laws and live with them. Infractions of the tax laws can result in the closure of your business, or fines, or imprisonment (or all three)—or at the very least, considerable bad publicity that you do not want as a businessowner in your community.

Other infractions that can affect your business reputation adversely are the failure to obtain the proper licenses and/or permits to operate your specific kind of business in your area. Be legal!

5

Despite your desire to begin a *small* business, the very nature of a building business makes even a small business a complex one. Not only should you, as owner-manager, have a working knowledge of the various skills of the building trades, you should also have at least a rudimentary knowledge of record keeping, business administration, legal matters pertaining to construction—and much more.

Certain management duties and problems are inherent to any kind of business, and a few management duties and problems are unique to the building business. The former require a general business knowledge, or the opportunity to enlist help from those who have this knowledge. The latter require specific technical knowledge, preferably backed by experience. As we have pointed out earlier, a lack of technical knowledge does not necessarily preclude success in the building business, but it does mean that you would have to hire—or acquire through a partnership—your expertise.

GENERAL ADMINISTRATION

The general administration of any business requires that you have an operational plan and a well thought-out method of implementing it. As applied to your specific business, this means that you have decided that your capital investment will allow you to operate as a custom builder, speculative builder, or repair/remodeling builder. You will know the general locality in which you wish to work, you will understand its housing and/or commercial building needs, and you will be familiar with its economic features, its suppliers and its financial institutions. You or your partners or employees will have the various skills that you will ultimately need to use on either a part- or full-time basis.

Personnel

As a small-business operator, your personnel needs will differ from those of the large operator only in that you will obtain certain services on a part-time basis. For general business purposes, you will need an accountant, an attorney, a secretary-typist, and a receptionist or telephone-answering service. For the technical aspects of your business, you will need employees skilled in the various phases of building that you intend for your firm to perform without the help of subcontractors. If you don't have a working familiarity with blueprints, mathematics as it applies to calculating material needs, or the operation of a surveyor's transit for leveling and squaring foundations, you will need employees skilled in these special tasks.

Once you have filled your personnel needs, you, or someone to whom you delegate authority, will see to it that each person understands his or her duties and responsibilities and what each can expect in the forms of wages and other benefits. Each person who represents your business, as either a full- or part-time employee, will understand what your company policies are regarding hours of work, break periods, customer relations, and quality of work. Each person will know exactly how much responsibility he or she can assume in making on-the-spot decisions when unforeseen conditions or emergencies arise.

Legal Matters

Legal matters that you will probably be called on to contend with are the writing of customer contracts, the obtaining of permits, licenses, etc., the drawing up of partnership agreements (if applicable), and any unforeseen matters unique to your particular circumstances.

Lawyers, like other professionals, come in various

degrees of competency. Learn as much as you can about the reputations for competency and efficiency of the lawyers of your area, since the one you choose will come to have access to many of the confidential details of your business. In the initial conference with a prospective lawyer, ask him if he has had experience in your particular area of business.

Purchasing

The careful buying of materials can increase your profits substantially. Know your suppliers, and know their policies regarding quality, pricing, and delivery. Learn as much as you can about sources of hard-to-get items of material, equipment, or tools—particularly if you live in a small town that is located rather far from major points of distribution. Establish some policy regarding the stocking of certain standard items of material. If you live where an inventory tax is applicable, you will want to time the stocking of materials to your best tax advantage.

Subcontracting

How many subcontractors are there in your area? How competent are they? How many jobs that you encounter will have to be done by subcontractors based outside your immediate area? No matter what phase of the building business you are in, you will probably be looked upon by the customer as the general contractor whose responsibility it is to find the most competent and reliable subcontractors available.

Design

You will have available a source of house designs suitable for your area or will have contact with an architectural firm that can help you with design, specifications, and other details.

Sales

Another of your managerial duties is to design—or have designed—an active sales program that fits your particular operation. Newspaper advertising will have to be discussed with the advertising manager of the newspaper. Display ads will have to be planned to include your company logo, slogan, business name, permanent address, and telephone number. Familiarize yourself with advertising space rates and discounts for sustained runs or increased space. Other advertising media are your local radio and regional television stations.

If you are a speculative builder, an important part of your sales effort can be taken over by trained salespersons or real estate brokers, who work on a straight commission, thus eliminating your need to maintain a salaried person for this service. Nevertheless, these people are part of your team and should be looked upon as such.

Financial Control

Financial management means that you are aware of, and know how to use, sources of loans. Such loans might be for equipment, land, material, or customer financing. To work intelligently in the area of finances, you should understand interest rates and how they are computed.

Construction

Good management on the construction end of your business means that you will supervise building starts to see that they are properly located, and discuss design, specifications, layout, zoning and building code requirements, material grades, timing of the entrance of subcontractors, etc., with your most trusted employee on the particular job. If, on the other hand, you let these important matters ''take care of themselves'' while you do the more menial work of digging ditches (or similar work), your business will be poorly managed.

Planning

Probably no one but yourself will be in a position to formulate long-range plans for your business format and future expansion. The day-by-day plans involving such matters as work schedules or the scheduling of new building starts might be turned over to a trusted employee or partner. However, whichever method you use, you should always know which plans are in execution and which are in abeyance.

All the duties that we have outlined may look as if they are too much for one person to perform. As a matter of fact, most successful managers constantly delegate authority and duties to others. But in the beginning, when you can't yet afford to hire skilled help in many different areas, you can improve your own management skills by study and practice. Pay attention when specialists (such as bankers and lawyers) make informative remarks. Learn the principles of such matters as interest computation and cost/sales ratios, and invest in one of the small, portable electronic calculators that you can take with you wherever you go.

Another good way to increase your managerial abilities is to take courses in management, if they are available in your area. Such courses are sometimes given under the joint sponsorship of the Small Business Administration and universities and/or community colleges. However, avoid becoming too deeply committed to such outside activities, at a time when your business needs full attention. It might be well, in fact, to take whatever courses that you feel are necessary for you before actually launching your business.

DECISION MAKING

Managers make decisions. Many decisions. Some of them are important decisions, some are relatively unimportant. Decision making is largely a psychological process, linked to such factors as your native intelligence, sense of self worth, background, etc. On one extreme of decision making are those persons who make snap decisions, and on the other are those persons who procrastinate when decisions have to be made. Although the proponents of both methods have much to say in their own favor, the best way to make decisions is undoubtedly *with an adequate input of the right kind of information.*

Where does information come from? It comes from many sources, both within and without your sphere of operations.

Information from Inside Sources

Your inside sources of information include the following:

Your Past Experience.   There is no doubt that those areas in which you have experience will be the easiest in which to make decisions. If your experience has been limited solely to technical operations, you can make decisions quickly and correctly in the technical area but will seek other sources for help in making business decisions.

Personal Observations.   Next to experience, your own personal observations are the most important input for making decisions. For example, your experience may tell you that, for all practical purposes, a concrete block foundation serves just as well as a poured concrete foundation; however, personal observation may reveal a distinct preference for the poured concrete foundation by customers in the area where you intend building. Your decision, in such a case, would be based upon this observation.

Employee Input.   Don't underestimate what employees might contribute to decision making. Even the quietest or most unobtrusive employee might have a wealth of experience in one particular phase of building, upon which you can profitably draw.

Cost Records.　Cost records, as they apply both to materials and to man-hours of labor on certain jobs, won't fully develop until after you've been in business for a while. When they are developed, study them closely as a reference for making future decisions.

Inventory Records.　It will be virtually compulsory that you keep inventory records for tax purposes, both federal and local. These inventory records can also guide you in making decisions regarding the purchase of various items as they relate to fiscal tax periods and price fluctuations.

Financial Reports.　Your in-company financial report will be derived from your bookkeeper and/or tax accountant and correlated to talks with your banker. Individuals and business entities alike are prone to overestimate their financial strength at crucial times. A periodic, thorough study of these financial reports will guide you in making decisions concerning expansion plans and the purchases of new equipment. And you will soon learn that your financial condition must always be judged with the tax angle in mind.

Personnel Records.　If circumstances dictate that you can't give a particular job your full attention, to which of your employees would you entrust the job?

An examination of personnel records will help you in making this decision. An employee's past employment record, illnesses, family responsibilities—all are factors to consider when deciding whether or not to delegate extra responsibility to him or her.

Progress Records. In the event that some projects have to be held in abeyance while others are allowed to proceed, which ones should they be? To make such decisions, you will need to thoroughly study the progress reports for all the projects that are under way.

From the foregoing, you can see that it is absolutely essential that a complete system of records and reports be worked out. Such a system should be thorough and constantly updated, with reports easily available in time to make important decisions. Employee job application blanks, designed to include as much information as possible, are a good basis for formulating personnel records. Worksheets on which each employee can record his or her daily activities, as well as materials used on specific jobs, provide a basis for both cost records and progress reports. Inventory records should be maintained on a continuing basis. Remember, information that takes too long to collect and prepare may not get to you until after the crucial time for making certain decisions has passed.

Information from Outside Sources

Your outside sources of information will include the following:

Architects' Plans and Specifications.   Any architect who submits plans and specifications for buildings in your area is quite likely completely knowledgeable concerning such matters as acceptable building design and zoning and building code requirements.

News Media.   Newspapers and radio and television broadcasts often include valuable information on local and regional building trends that will help you in making decisions. These sources also provide some information on past, present, and future economic trends that might affect building starts in your area.

Product Information and Price Quotations.   To properly manage a business, you must maintain a constant balance between expenses and income. One of the major factors in expenses is the cost of materials. Lumber suppliers are usually in a position to predict future price fluctuations, and any information that they can give you regarding material costs should become a part of your decision-making data. You should also be able to get from suppliers information on changes in grades, styles, and availability of materials.

Observation of Local Conditions.   You should be constantly aware of local conditions that apply to your business. Local trends do not always accurately reflect regional or national ones. A myriad of factors can affect local building; among them are: (1) the availability of water, (2) the local capacity for handling sewage, (3) the effects of local zoning laws on certain types of building. There are others. For example, local authorities may be contemplating a moratorium on building until funds are available to update the city's sewage system. Sources of this kind of information are newspaper accounts and especially your own personal contacts with commissioners, the city manager, local planning boards, and other governmental sources.

General Economic Data.　　In perhaps no other industry are general economic changes reflected so quickly and dramatically as in the building industry. Changes in interest rates, or in the policies of lending institutions, will set up a ripple of effects that are felt first and most profoundly in building on the local level. For example, it would be foolish to plan a great many speculative housing starts at a time when loans for home buyers were becoming difficult to get. The best source of information on home financing is from bankers and savings and loan officers.

PLANNING

Inherent in virtually every successful operation is a long-range plan for achieving some major business goal. To implement this long-range plan, there will be many short-range plans which should lead to minor goals, or *subgoals*. The long-range planning is important—almost imperative—but many businessmen do question the usefulness of putting a great deal of time and energy into short-range planning, which can seriously limit the flexibility of a business operation. Probably the best that can be said for short-range planning is that the resourceful businessman does just enough of it to prevent circumstances from dictating the direction in which the business will go. But, like the player in any kind of game, he keeps his eyes always on the long-range goal, toward which the long-range plan is to take him.

One aspect of short-range planning that is important is scheduling. The cost of labor precludes carrying a job to completion in a haphazard manner, with no consideration to the scheduling of its various phases. Therefore, each step of each job should be scheduled—from the day when a surveyor goes in with a transit to lay out the foundation to the day the final trim is installed in the completed house.

To effectively schedule a job, it should be divided into stages of completion, with a construction timetable worked out that will fit the job. To implement the timetable, you will need a control chart that will show the progress and type of work that is currently underway on each job. By correlating these three visual elements—the timetable, the control chart and the appearance of the job itself—you should know immediately if a job is progressing on time and according to schedule; if it is not, you should make adjustments immediately, thereby avoiding costly delays in progress.

So important is the scheduling of production that it is the central step in coordinating all the various elements of your business. The proper coordination of the enterprise starts at the very beginning, with the obtaining of just the right number of contracts and/or speculative projects so that all of your resources—

including labor, equipment, and materials—are used to their fullest advantage at all times. The danger, of course, is in making so many commitments that you can't fulfill them on time. And such coordination must be continued in all phases of the enterprise, allowing you to begin new contracts as previous ones are fulfilled. Or, in the case of the speculative builder, you will have a coordinated sales plan for selling houses quickly enough that your cash flow will not be tied up in unsold houses.

THE AVAILABILITY OF MATERIAL AND SUBCONTRACTORS

While you may not have all the control over the scheduling of subcontractors that you would like, you'll have to make every effort to properly schedule subcontracted work. To accomplish this, you may have to incorporate some flexibility into your schedules so as to keep your own employees working productively even though a subcontractor can't or won't schedule his activities to coincide with yours.

The availability of material when you need it is also an important factor in job scheduling. The method you use to ensure the availability of material will depend upon such a factor as the reliability of suppliers. You may, for example, have to sacrifice the savings that can be made through orders from distant suppliers in favor of the more reliable service you can get on a local basis. Your methods of buying will depend to some extent upon how big your operation is and how much material you can afford to carry in inventory.

Many small builders deal exclusively with local suppliers to be assured of getting what they want, when they want it.

THE IMPORTANCE OF YOUR WORK FORCE

There are extremely few enterprises that can be run singlehandedly, or that can be operated efficiently without close cooperation between the operator and the people who work for him.

The first step in getting a crew with whom you can work in close cooperation is in the proper screening and selection of prospective employees. After that, you must do all that you can to develop the talent and ability of each individual employee, for it is only through well-qualified workers that you can shift attention from the many minor details of building to good management techniques.

As your business grows and becomes more complex, you'll see the advantages to be gained in turning over part of the management to some qualified employee. In fact, most highly successful business managers attribute their success not so much to luck or hard work as to their ability to choose and train employees and use them to their fullest potential. This includes delegating authority and important tasks to them.

The Building Crew

Despite the fact that there always seems to be considerable unemployment, finding skilled and competent workers to hire is not always easy. You can have the free service of the United States Employment Service office as well as the paid services of private employment agencies in finding workers. A want-ad run in your local newspaper may bring results. Such sources, combined with your familiarity with the workers of your area, should give you the necessary contacts for hiring employees.

Even if you hire only part-time employees, you will accept certain obligations for them, as well as certain rights and duties when and if you lay them off. To understand your obligations, rights, and duties in regard to hiring workers, consult with your lawyer.

Both you and your employees will have a more profitable relationship if you can keep enough work lined up to maintain a full-time work crew that can learn to work as a team. Layoffs can be costly to both you and your employees, and there is always the risk of permanently losing the availability of competent workers when you lay them off.

The Office Crew

Even in the beginning you will have many tasks for someone who can do secretarial and record-keeping duties and take phone messages. At first, this person may be your wife or some other family member, but as your business grows you should hire an experienced, career-oriented person who can be the key to a smoothly functioning office crew when and if your business demands it. Just as with your work crew, you should choose office help with an eye to delegating as much responsibility and authority to them as possible.

OCCUPATIONAL INJURIES

When you hire a worker, you are to some extent responsible for his or her on-the-job safety. In fact, worker-accidents are a major problem of American industry: the U.S. Department of Labor has estimated the cost to employers of occupational injuries in a single recent year to be over $3.5 billion. And in the same period, the cost of the occupational injuries to the accident victims themselves was an estimated $1.4 billion, without considering the cost in human suffering and grief. The following yearly averages, compiled over a ten-year period, will give you some idea of the extent of that suffering and grief:

- Annually, an average of over 17,000 workers are killed or totally disabled for life.
- Annually, an average of over 83,000 workers are partially disabled for life.
- Annually, an average of approximately 2 million workers are temporarily disabled.

Certain industries are rated as high-hazard industries, and the construction industry is one of them. Since you are legally required to pay into the fund that recompenses your injured workers, it will pay you in actual dollars and cents to maintain some kind of safety program. For a small business, this would not have to be a comprehensive program, with safety awards, etc., but you should foster an awareness within your organization that you expect workers to follow safe work practices. It will be your responsibility to see that all of your equipment is maintained in safe operating condition and that workers do not remove safety devices from the machines. You may even require that the workers wear certain items of safety apparel, such as hard hats or safety glasses.

METHODS ANALYSIS

Many large businesses find that it is profitable to conduct time studies relative to working methods, from which they learn how many workers to place on a particular job to do that job most efficiently. You know, of course, that three men working on a job will finish the job more quickly than two men, but what about the comparison of total man-hours devoted to that job in such a comparison? Whichever method produces a given amount of work in the least man-hours is the most efficient method and, generally speaking, the one that should be used.

The best way to conduct your own time study is to time a job with a stopwatch as it is performed by various methods. When a variety of jobs are timed in this manner and the data are recorded on a time-study sheet, you will have valuable information regarding the scheduling of jobs, as well as a cost record of the various phases of carrying a job to completion.

6

Selling Yourself, Your Services, and Your Product

I t is axiomatic in American business today that having an excellent product or service to sell is only half the battle—the other half is *selling it*. Some companies build good sales records on seemingly little advertising other than their own reputation, and this may be your goal in the building business. But it takes a long time to establish such a reputation, particularly in a field as competitive as building. Furthermore, once your good reputation is established, the competition doesn't quit and may, in fact, grow keener. Therefore, you should very soon learn to think of selling as a continuous effort, one that will require not only effort on your own part but an advertising budget as well.

Advertising comes in many forms, except, unfortunately, a form that is *free*. Word-of-mouth advertising is often looked upon as free advertising, but it has the major drawback of being unreliable. Moreover, a certain amount of effort must go into establishing an advertising program that travels by word-of-mouth, and when this same amount of effort is translated into dollars, the advertising can no longer be looked upon as free. Other forms of advertising are (1) media advertising, (2) direct advertising, either through salespeople or by direct mail or a combination of both, and (3) participation in community projects.

If your building activities include speculative building, advertising and selling will be a major part of your business. In this case, you will probably use both media and direct advertising as an aid to selling. Whether you use your own salespeople or sell your houses through a real estate broker, there will be expenses to consider.

If you specialize in remodeling and repair—or use it to supplement your other building activities—an aggressive and continuing sales effort will certainly be needed. It is the nature of remodeling and repair that a reputation for reliability and quality work is extremely important, so that these intangibles become a part of your selling effort.

As a custom builder you may have less expense in media advertising and will probably require no direct salespeople at all. In custom building, much of your advertising will be on a more professional basis, through contacts with such other professionals as architects, who will have you on their list of bidders. Your reputation, which you will develop through both your work and your customer relations, will be important. Nevertheless, even in the field of custom building, you will find a need for some active selling, which may take the form of a moderate amount of media advertising and/or participation in projects that create goodwill toward you in your community. For example, you might think about sponsoring a Little League baseball team or a scholarship to send a student to college.

THE COST OF ADVERTISING

The cost of advertising, as related to gross income, varies widely from business to business. The paradox of the matter is that the new business, with the relatively small gross income, really needs the relatively larger advertising budget to build business. To complicate the problem, the returns from advertising are often tenuous and difficult to calculate. Thus, the newcomer to the business is often in a quandary: How much advertising is too little? How much is enough? How much is too much? Does advertising *pay* or does it simply *cost*?

To answer these questions, we can say that a sensible advertising program, geared to your own particular income potential, should *pay*, but it may take some time before you realize returns from it. A figure that is often quoted as a guideline for the building business is that an advertising budget should be two percent of gross income. However, it would seem that few builders, particularly in higher income brackets, actually spend that much on advertising. On the other side of the income spectrum is the small company with limited capital to allocate to an advertising budget. But when your firm is new, you will have even more need than the established firm for a well-planned and well-organized campaign to sell yourself, your products, and your services. The advertising dollars that you spend now may come back to you when they are badly needed.

For the same reason that you don't turn the electrical wiring of a house over to one of your carpenters, you shouldn't attempt to run the highly specialized activity of an intensive selling campaign yourself. Selling—that is, successful selling—is a job for the promotion specialist. To pay for this kind of help in the beginning might seem like an extravagance, but a competent specialist in sales promotions can develop a sales campaign that will bring better results and cost less money than one you could develop yourself. A specialist can advise you where, when, and how to advertise; compose ad layouts for newspaper advertising or copy for radio and television; and advise you on the relationship between your gross income and advertising costs.

Custom builders and repair/remodeling builders usually find the problems of effective advertising more easily solved than does the speculative builder. Most custom and repair/remodeling builders do their advertising in newspapers, on radio and television, and through personal contacts. The speculative builder works in a more complex marketplace and has more complex advertising needs. Therefore, the remainder of this chapter deals with the advertising, selling, and merchandising problems you will encounter if you engage in speculative building. And, in the broader sense, some of the points that we cover will be of help to you as a custom builder or repair/re-modeling builder.

Planning Construction and Sales

The three cardinal rules to be observed in the building of salable houses are (1) build houses in the right location, (2) build houses of the proper design, floor plan, and style to suit the market that you are aiming for, and (3) build a house that can be priced appropriately.

For the speculative builder, this means that the selling of a house begins with the correct selection of a building site. For example, if you plan to exploit a housing market that consists of young, working-class couples with children, you should look for moderate-to low-cost land that is easily accessible to schools or school bus routes. The designs, floor plans, and styles of the houses would be appropriate to the sites and to the market consisting of young, working-class couples with children. Even the technical details of construction, the utilities, and landscaping would be planned with this market in mind. With these goals set from the outset, the pricing of the house for the income group that you are aiming for becomes automatic, and you should have a package with sales appeal.

Know Your Market.   As we have pointed out earlier, the problems of producing an item are often not as complex as those of selling the item once it is produced. This is because your experience, equipment, technology, and material are all oriented toward production, but not necessarily toward merchandising. Therefore, as a speculative builder, before you even begin to analyze the problems of production, you should study your potential market. Examine it with the following points in mind.

1. The general economic outlook for:
    a. The *region* in which you will be building. If the primary industry of that region is farming, for example, what is the general outlook for farming? Has any recent state or federal legislation been enacted that will affect the farming industry? Have serious droughts been forecast for the near future?
    b. The *state* in which you will be building. The economic figures for your state should be easily available. These figures will reflect the unemployment rate, as compared with that of other states and with the national average; the potential of the state for attracting new industries, grants-in-aid from the federal government, and other sources of growth; the potential of the state for attracting new residents in the form of immigrants from other states, who need to be provided with housing.
    c. The *community* in which you will be building. The economic outlook of a community may be tied directly to that of its state or region, or, because of certain well-established industries or natural resources, it may be economically autonomous. Ask yourself the following questions: How are most people of the community employed? What is the predomi-

nant wage level? What are the prospects that new industry will be attracted to the community—or that established industries will be lost? Has the housing market of the community been traditionally strong, or traditionally weak?

2. The kinds of houses with the best sales appeal. When this is analyzed on a local basis, you will probably see that there is a regional connection, insofar as style and design are concerned. You might also discover a distinct preference in certain communities for certain kinds of material. For example, communities that depend upon the logging and lumber industry for their economic strength are traditionally heavy users of wood products in residential building, whereas in communities that rely on the manufacture of cement or concrete aggregate, the use of concrete blocks might be indicated—or at least acceptable—for residential building.

3. The price range most acceptable to the largest number of potential buyers. The optimum price range of homes in a community should correlate with the predominant income level. However, if certain unusual circumstances prevail—such as a predominantly low-income community with a housing market already glutted with low-income housing—you may have to study the possibility of building houses that are priced within the range of a certain fringe group.

4. The *kinds* of people that you expect as potential buyers. Is the population of the community stable or largely transient? What are the traditional

methods used to get customer financing? Are the potential customers the kind who traditionally take pride in home ownership, thus creating a healthy housing market in which financing is usually available? Are they predominantly people of rural origin who would appreciate space for a garden, or are they largely urban oriented, preferring relatively small lots with paved driveways and minimal outside work? Are there usually several wage earners in each family?

5. The zoning of the community as it pertains to the kinds of houses that you plan to build. Are building sites in fact available in the area in which the kinds of houses that you plan to build would be most appropriate?

6. The activities of your competitors. One of the most significant advantages that a competitor can gain over you is that of offering financing to customers. Ask yourself these questions: What financing do my competitors offer their customers? What kind of financing can I offer?

Deciding on the Type of House to Build.   The first house that you build will undoubtedly be planned to sell within a narrow price range, which will to some extent determine the type of house that you build. Nevertheless, even a restricted price range will allow some variations in style, design, kinds of material, etc. Again, the kind of market that you are working into will do more to influence your decision on what type of house to build than will the price range. To make these tactical construction detail decisions intelligently, you should consider the market demands carefully, remembering that once you have committed yourself to a particular type of house, it will be difficult to change your plans. Consider the following questions:

1. How many rooms will the houses have? This is usually interpreted as, How many bedrooms? since considerable emphasis is placed upon having enough bedrooms for the various members of the family. Three-bedroom homes are extremely popular on the premise that they will serve either a small or moderate-sized family. Retirees on small, fixed incomes often want two-bedroom homes. Homes with one bedroom are seldom built. Homes with more than three bedrooms usually fall into a different price class than three-bedroom homes.

2. How many square feet will the houses contain? The liveable area of a house is an important selling point. Houses of a given price should be kept within a given range of area.

3. Will the houses have single or double garages? Double garages also offer strong selling points for a house. Growing families feel that they need a double garage (sometimes with the thought of eventually remodeling a portion of it into a family room); retirees like to use the extra garage space for storage or a shop.

4. What appliances will be included with the house? Appliances include a range, refrigerator, washer and dryer, garbage disposal unit, dish washer, and possibly a built-in vacuum cleaning unit. The *quality* of such items should also be considered, since their quality can reflect upon your competence as a builder in the customer's mind.

5. What style of architecture will be used in the houses? The architectural design of the houses must be regionally acceptable or popular, as well as appropriate to the neighborhood where the houses are to be located.
6. Will the houses be constructed of wood, brick, concrete block—or some other material? Will they be prefabricated? Precut? Will they have roofs of tar and gravel, composition shingles, wood shingles, or shakes?
7. Will trees, shrubs, lawns, and landscaping be included as a part of the housing package?

The Federal Housing Administration annually issues reports containing information that is useful in deciding what type of houses to build. The reports are available at your local FHA insuring offices.

Deciding How Many Houses to Build.   In deciding how many houses to build initially, you will have to answer basic questions: (1) How much area in building sites is available? (2) How many houses will my finances allow me to build initially? (3) How many houses can I expect to sell in a length of time that will not keep my money tied up dangerously long?

The last question is correlated to market conditions. If the housing market in the style and price range of the houses that you have decided to build is not particularly brisk, you should proceed cautiously, perhaps with two or three houses at the start. If you are working into a strong housing market, with ample building sites available, you may plan to build twenty—or more—houses a year. For such a number of houses, your best bet would probably be to begin with five or six houses, in a variety of styles, to serve as showplace houses.

If you are fortunate enough to have the finances, the building sites, and the market potential to justify the building of twenty or more houses in a year, you will be in a position to develop long-range planning, or a year-long building schedule. You then could develop an extremely efficient schedule, and retain good workers on a year-round basis. On the other side of the coin, if you miscalculate the long-range market potential, commitments that you can't get out of could lead to financial disaster. Any long-range building schedule should be hedged with safety factors that would allow changes in case of changing market conditions.

THE PROBLEMS OF SELLING

Generally speaking, the housing market is competitive enough that you will have to *merchandise* and *promote* your product. If you don't turn this phase of your business over to specialists, you will have to plan and execute your own merchandising and promotion campaign. The ways in which you can implement such a campaign are with (1) exhibit homes, (2) material exhibits, (3) an advertising program, and (4) a direct sales program.

The Showplace Home

Your first showplace home will be a prototype of that particular type and style of house. It should, of course, be complete to the last detail, including land-scaping and furnishings, with the furnishings chosen to complement the style and color of the house. You should be able to get a local furniture store to provide the furnishings as a form of advertisement, with the agreement that if the house is sold with the furnishings, the store will be reimbursed. If your long-range goal is to use your own salespeople to sell all the houses that you build in the future, you may use a small amount of space in the house as the salesperson's office. Even this office should be appropriately located to suggest to prospective customers that the house is designed to provide space for a home office.

Material Exhibits

Material exhibits should be placed in strategic locations around the house. Ideally, these exhibits should show the hidden quality that is built into the house, quality that the customer does not normally see, or may not understand unless it is pointed out. For example, a cutaway section showing the construction details of an outside wall of the house, complete with studding, vapor barrier, siding, insulation, and interior sheathing and finish, would make an effective display. Other material displays, such as the soil pipe used by the plumber or the conduit or cable used by the electrician, should be available from either the suppliers or the subcontractors themselves.

To call the customers' attention to the various construction and material displays, small signs should be placed around the house. It would also be a good idea to provide maps showing the location of the house in relation to schools, shopping centers, churches, public transportation, city parks, main thoroughfares, and so on.

Advertising

Not only does money have to be spent on a selling campaign, it must be spent wisely. Several different media can be used for advertising your product.

Newspaper Space. Most business-oriented people rely heavily on newspaper advertising. Newspaper advertising space can be classed as either *display advertising* or *classified advertising*. Display advertising requires a certain amount of artwork, which can usually be provided in the form of stock art (art already prepared that covers building in a general way) or custom art (art produced by an artist, usually to your specifications). The ad layout expert of the newspaper will explain your art needs for display advertising to you and should be able to provide suitable stock art. Other sources of stock art are available in the form of brochures furnished by your suppliers. However, be sure to receive permission from the company publishing the brochure before using any portions of it in your own advertising.

Classified advertising is usually used to follow up display advertising. Whereas display ads are usually placed on a one-time or short-term basis, classified advertising is thought to be more effective when run on a repeated or sustained basis.

How much do you spend on newspaper advertising? Many builders believe that about half of your entire advertising budget should be allocated to newspaper advertising, with the remainder being divided between other forms of advertising.

One form of newspaper advertising that is free, if you learn how and when to use it, is a news release. The premise of the news release as a form of advertising is that anything that you do in your business that is newsworthy has the potential for being published as a *news story*. In many cases, newsworthy stories don't find their ways into the newspaper simply because the local newspapers are not adequately staffed to ferret out and write the copy for them. You stand a fair chance of getting the advantage of this kind of free advertising if you notify your newspaper when your activities are newsworthy. If this fails to get action, try preparing your own news release and personally give it to your local newspaper editor.

Which newspapers do you use for advertising? Regional coverage will be provided by your metropolitan newspaper, of course. If you are conducting business in a small town, you will probably have access to small-town newspapers, usually published on a weekly basis, that can give you the kind of coverage you need. You may consider the possibility of using the weekly newspapers of two or three neighboring small towns to advertise your houses.

Signs.   Signs are an effective way of advertising, if they can be located near a well-traveled route. You will have to obtain permission to place signs in areas other than your own sites.

Brochures. Brochures may be effective, especially if they are carefully planned, with the aid of the graphic arts people at your printer's. You can give each person whom you contact, or each person who visits your exhibit homes, a brochure. This person is in turn very likely to show the brochure to friends, with the result that each brochure that you distribute will be seen by two or more people. A brochure may actually have more residual impact than newspaper advertising, inasmuch as it may be recalled to someone's attention weeks or months after it is initially distributed.

Direct Mail Advertising. Direct mail advertising is sometimes used by builders. One of the single largest expenses of direct mail advertising is the cost of postage, and you should consult with your postmaster about the possibility of making bulk mailings by third-class mail, which is less expensive than first class. You should have a thorough understanding of the requirements of the postal service as they apply to the use of various postal rates before setting up your order for printed envelopes with the printer.

Selling

One of the tactical decisions that you will have to make in the early planning stages is whether you will handle the actual selling of the houses yourself or use the services of a real estate broker. Some advantages of using a real estate broker are:
1. The broker knows the local housing market.

2. The broker has—or should have—experience in sales and promotions of houses.
3. The broker has access to more sales contacts than you have.
4. Because the broker is in the business of selling houses in a wide range of prices and styles, he or she naturally attracts more prospective customers than you can.
5. Just as you have a work force trained in building a house smoothly and efficiently, the broker has a trained sales force to handle the details of selling smoothly and efficiently.
6. The broker understands the legalities of selling property.
7. Since the broker works on a commission, you will have no expenses connected with selling until sales are made.

The disadvantages of using a broker are:

1. The broker may look upon your house as just another item on the sales list and not concentrate effort on selling it as you would.
2. The commission that you pay the broker is money that you can well use.

It is obvious that the advantages of using a broker outweigh the disadvantages. Therefore, you should be willing to turn over this selling job, which takes time and effort, to an experienced real estate broker, thus leaving yourself more time for the work that you can do best. Nevertheless, there are many pros and cons to consider when deciding whether or not to do your own selling. It is a decision to be made by the individual builder, after reviewing all the factors of individual circumstances.

7

Bookkeeping for a Purpose: To "Keep Score"

Few businesses have been operated successfully without a system of bookkeeping, which involves, on your part, the systematic keeping of records. With a system of record keeping and bookkeeping, you are likely to succeed; without it you are likely to fail.

To keep records properly, you must devote some space to the facilities needed for them. It is much better if the space you decide to use as an office is devoted exclusively to those activities associated with your business. Even an office located in your home will be more functional if devoted exclusively to your business, and in such a case it will be an allowable business expense deduction (under the current ruling) for income tax purposes.

Ideally, an office should be large enough that customers can visit you there. If this precludes the use of a home office, you will be looking for office space elsewhere. But in the beginning, a home office with minimal furnishings and equipment may serve the purpose.

THE OFFICE CREW

There are many ways to recruit office help. One of the more popular ways is to press your spouse into service with the expectation that she will take care of correspondence, phone calls, and routine record keeping. If your wife is inexperienced or too busy with family duties, you may be better off hiring a qualified, experienced person to keep records on a part-time basis and using a telephone answering service to take your phone calls. Usually, records are given over to a bookkeeping service periodically to be kept in such a manner that they could be studied by a tax auditor, if one should ever demand to see them.

Regardless of whom you recruit as office help, he or she should be able to work faithfully, for the required number of hours weekly, to keep a comprehensive set of records with which the bookkeeper can work. These records form the basis for providing information about one of your most pressing problems: cash flow.

A PURPOSE FOR THE RECORDS

Keep your day-by-day records as *simple* as possible and yet as *complete* as possible. For your own part of this effort, you must obtain and save every receipt for all purchases relating to your business. Never fail to record the amount of each business-related check that you write. When you purchase items of equipment, the invoice must be retained so that your bookkeeper will have a date and figure upon which to begin a depreciation schedule on that particular piece of equipment.

The second step in the record keeping is to record the information that you provide, in a system that is complete enough to allow you to make up annual operating and financial statements of profit and loss, as well as balance sheets. We have already pointed out the need for keeping adequate tax records. Your records will also show the officers of banks and savings and loan organizations the financial health of your company, in the event that you should want to borrow money.

SCHEDULING YOUR CASH FLOW

As a businessman, it is imperative that you establish a good record of paying your bills when they are due. To do this, you must have cash on hand with which to meet your ongoing obligations. By the time you have set up a system of record keeping, you will have learned how to make an estimate of your cash needs. Your record keeping—with the help of an accountant—should provide a system that will allow you to see at a glance how much cash you have on hand.

Every cash receipt and every expenditure should be

recorded, as part of your routine office work, in a journal or on a ledger sheet. Your accountant should be able to help you set up a simple system of record keeping.

BOOKKEEPING

To make the final bookkeeping as systematic and useful as possible, the journal or ledger sheet transactions should be classified and distributed among various accounts. Thus, the entries are divided into several sections, according to the type of account, such as: asset accounts; liability accounts; net worth accounts; and income and expense accounts. This is the information that is the basis of your profit and loss statements and balance sheets.

RECORDING JOB COSTS

Every item of receipts and expenses that you enter in a system of records should carry some identification, so that they may be charged to the proper account for the purpose of analyzing job costs. For example, the exact number of 2 × 4 studs that you use on a specific job should be interpreted into dollars and cents and charged to that specific job. The gasoline that you use in your vehicle while overseeing the entire operation will be charged to a general overhead account, as will your office rent, the general maintenance expenses on equipment, etc.

Labor costs should be allocated to the specific jobs

on which they are incurred. If there is any question concerning the relationship between a materials billing and the job on which the material was used, you might ask your supplier to indicate the designation of the material on the invoice. Material taken from your own stockpile will have to be computed separately, based upon its price at the time of purchase. To do this, you will have to carry a pocket notebook in which to make field records for your record keeper's use.

The cost of subcontracting should be relatively easy to record, providing the subcontractor bills you for each individual job. If you get a statement for work done on a group of houses, you will have to break the statement down according to the expense incurred on each house, in order to maintain a cost record of each house.

Analyzing Job Costs

To properly analyze the cost of each job, you will need to know (1) the total cost of each job, and (2) the amount of the general overhead generated by each job. To obtain these figures, you will have to identify each cost item, check each item against the quantities received on the building site and correlate these costs to the original estimates made on the job. If the actual cost is significantly out of line with the original estimates, this is a signal to investigate the reasons for the discrepancy.

To compile a record of the labor to be charged to each job, your foreman will keep a daily record of hours that each worker spends on each job. The time should be charged, not only to a specific job, but also to a specific task on that job. A cost analysis of this kind will be invaluable in planning cash flow as well as in making future estimates.

Payroll Records

It is absolutely imperative that you keep records of the number of hours worked each day by each of your employees. Not only is this cost an important business expense for both your profit-and-loss records and income tax records, it is also information that must be used to compute the employee's wages, withholding tax, FICA tax, and so on. These records must be retained for a period of time, in case any dispute should arise concerning the amount the employee was paid, or for possible future tax audits. Your accountant can advise you on how to set up these records and how long they should be retained. The maintenance of these records is a legal obligation.

Using the Records

The importance of keeping records cannot be overemphasized. Many business owners have a tendency in the early stages of a business to neglect to retain invoices and keep records on certain transactions, thinking that they will "get around to it later." But as they get busier and busier with the details of building, they get further and further from establishing a systematic method of record keeping. This results in a condition in which the businessman has no knowledge about the most vital concern of the business—its profit-and-loss status. Furthermore, the owner would not be able to supply tax records on demand by the state or federal tax departments, which could result in disputed income tax returns at a future time when they were least anticipated.

Unless you really understand and enjoy the paperwork involved in keeping a comprehensive set of books, you will be better off to turn over this important task to an experienced bookkeeper on a part-time basis. The bookkeeper should be able to explain the financial condition of your firm to you at any given time.

The fact of having a bookkeeper, however, does not absolve you of the need to study and analyze your records periodically. A study of them should show you

1. if overhead expenses should be cut.
2. if employees are being scheduled efficiently.
3. if materials are being purchased and used properly.
4. if payroll taxes are being handled in the prescribed manner.
5. if all obligations are being met promptly.
6. if the relationship between gross income and business expenses is such that
   a. your firm is showing the required percentage of profit.
   b. you are taking advantage of all the legal tax breaks that are available to you as a business owner.
7. the relationship between your assets and liabilities.

It might serve a useful purpose to take certain of

your key employees into your confidence regarding company records. One way to do this is to hold periodic meetings, either weekly, biweekly or monthly, to discuss the profit-and-loss status of your firm. The feedback from key employees is important data for planning improvements in work methods, utilization of materials, scheduling of workers, and other operational details.

8

Designing and Building a House

f and when your building activities come to include the building of custom or speculative houses, you will be aware of the importance of design and architectural quality. This is, of course, especially true in speculative building; but even in custom building you are in a position to suggest a design to your prospective customer that would be most suitable to his or her needs and wants.

The problems of house design become more complex as you realize that, not only must you design a house with as much inherent quality as is possible in its price range, it must also appeal to the customer, who may be more impressed with certain superficialities of design than with inherent quality. This customer appeal becomes of paramount importance in the design of speculative houses, in which a seeming

119

design defect, or a variation from the norm, could be a fatal mistake at selling time.

Design and architectural considerations bring up the question, Do you design your own or secure the services of others? To answer this question, you should first have a general understanding of what goes into the planning and design of a house.

1. First, there is the basic design of the house to consider. This design encompasses the architectural details that profoundly influence the outward appearance of the house, which is the all-important factor in customer appeal.

2. After a design is chosen, a complete set of plans and specifications must be drawn up. These plans and specifications serve a variety of purposes, including the important one of providing a schematic representation that will show the appropriate lending institutions and agencies (banks, savings and loans, FHA, VA) that the house is planned in accordance with building codes and lending requirements.

3. The plot plan must be developed and the house sited on the lot. This implies a knowledge of the format of the streets and utilities in the area, as well as some consideration of climatic conditions that could affect the siting of the house.

4. Next, the foundation of the house must be laid out in such a manner that the workers will be able to maintain the floors level, and the walls true and square, with a minimum of adjustments. This initial layout is usually done with a surveyor's transit, with which corners and elevations are established and designated with stakes and chalk lines. This is done not only for the benefit of your own

workers but also for the benefit of subcontractors, who will take it for granted that you have correctly marked corners and elevations.

5. Finally, you—or your foreman—will oversee construction to make sure that the workers adhere to the plans and specifications that are such an important part of the overall job. This supervision would also include keeping an eye on the subcontractors to be sure that they also adhere to plans and specifications, including the use of materials that will meet building code requirements.

DESIGNING THE HOUSE

With an understanding of what is involved in the design of the house, you will be able to determine whether you or someone else will produce the house design. A few builders in fact do their own designing, but the general consensus of opinion among most builders is that this is a specialized activity, requiring architectural and engineering training, as well as considerable time that might be better spent in actual construction. These builders prefer to use the various design services that are available, such as:

Architectural Firms

A local architectural firm can undoubtedly provide you with house designs of the best quality, which will meet all the building codes as well as zoning—and other—regulations. It would in fact be inconceivable that a reputable architect would not supply you with

architectural designs that would exceed the requirements of most local zoning regulations and building
codes. However, designs from an architectural firm
are usually expensive, perhaps more so than can be
justified by the price range of the houses that you will
build. In that case, your recourse is to use a less expensive design service.

Architects' Multiple Plans

Architects, much like artists, make up portfolios of
house designs for various types of houses. You can
get copies of these designs at considerably less cost
than a commissioned design. You may have some
trouble in finding designs to suit your specific purposes, but if they are available, these kinds of architects' plans are useful.

Suppliers' Designs

If you plan to use prefabricated components, the
suppliers of these components may furnish you with
designs and plans. However, you may still need the
services of a surveyor or engineer in surveying the
building site and adapting the house to local building
codes and regulations.

House Design Services

There are various house plan services available that
provide collections of designs, complete with plans
and specifications. These are usually satisfactory for

houses in a moderate price range, providing that they meet with the approval of the various lending institutions and agencies from whom the prospective buyer will obtain a loan.

In any case, the style of the houses that you build should conform to the established styles of the area and region in which you build. You may be tempted, for the sake of uniqueness, to deviate from the established standard, but the deviation must be thought out with care. And in no case should you risk building many houses that are unique or different in design, since changing the public's tastes is an extremely risky business.

Custom Features

Although sameness in design can force you into an unimaginative position in architecture, the inclusion of *custom features* can, from the customer's viewpoint, offer some uniqueness. These special features might include covered patios or circular driveways (where space will allow); and inside the house, you might incorporate special bathroom fixtures, such as an additional shower head positioned low enough to be used from a sitting position. Many times the special features can be worked into the basic design of a house with but little added expense, and they can greatly enhance the sales appeal of the house.

Split-Level and Storied Houses

Inherent in the basic design of a house are the number of functional floor levels that it contains. Generally, the decision to build split-level houses will depend upon the terrain, and they are most adaptable to a hilly terrain. Storied houses, which can be built on level terrain, should be appropriate to the area, the requirements of lot space, and so on.

The All-Important Bedrooms

Perhaps the first part of a house that the mother of a growing family looks at is the space for sleeping. Almost invariably, the growing family will require at least three bedrooms, with four- and five-bedroom houses becoming extremely popular. Often, the same basic floor space can be partitioned in such a manner as to provide additional—but relatively smaller— bedrooms, thus increasing the sales appeal of the house.

Thinking of the Man of the Family

While the woman of the house eyes the bedrooms, and possibly the kitchen, the typical man will have an eye for either shop space or office space (or both), depending upon what he does with his leisure time. If such amenities can't be included within the price range of the house, you should use a house design that is versatile enough that certain space (such as the double garage or additional bedroom) can be easily modified by the customer after he moves in. For example, garages can be designed so that standard size, easily available windows replace garage doors with a minimum of do-it-yourself carpentry.

Appliances and Utilities Fixtures

Certain items of utilities equipment (such as furnaces for central heating systems) are considered standard items with the new house, while certain others (such as refrigerators and ranges) are considered extras. The inclusion of a dishwasher and/or garbage disposal unit in the original plans will save the customer the later trouble of having them installed. The inclusion of such extras would give you two important advantages: (1) by buying in fairly large quantities, you could get a better price break on these major appliances than your customer could, and (2) if the cost of some major appliances can be included in the sales price of the house, it will make a more attractive deal for the customer.

The disadvantage of your including major appliances—aside from the obvious one that it increases your production costs—is that if an appliance proves to be defective or a chronic troublemaker, the customer will blame you as readily as the manufacturer or supplier of the appliance.

Landscaping

Just as an attractive display enhances the salability of an item displayed in a shop, an attractive landscape around a house enhances its salability. This does not mean that you, the builder, should provide a fully grown lawn and flowering shrubs around a new house, but you should do enough landscaping, along with minimal planting, so that mud and dust around the house will be held to a minimum and the general overall outer appearance of the property is improved.

CONSTRUCTION

When all the planning is completed and actual construction begun, you will have to have a firm grasp of construction details.

Systematized Construction

Most experienced builders systematize the construction of houses to the extent that it is possible. For example, if a builder decides to build a certain type of foundation (let's say a concrete block foundation, as opposed to a poured concrete foundation), he will use that same kind of foundation for each and every house, thereby developing a routine that the workers can follow for maximum efficiency. When the masonry work is brought to a point where the hollow blocks are ready for grouting, the builder will order enough mixed concrete to grout all the foundations in a continuous operation. As construction progresses to various other stages, the material, along with workers who are specialists in that particular phase of building, will be available to carry the entire project to completion as quickly as possible. This procedure eliminates time losses that would otherwise result while carpenters and helpers were changing from one tool to the other or readjusting their thoughts and motions to new activities.

By close and accurate scheduling of the various stages in the construction of a house, systematized construction principles have been applied to the construction of a single house, on a demonstration basis, so that the entire house—exclusive of the foundation but including the plumbing, electrical work, and installation of the heating system—was completed in one day.

To systematize construction, you can do the following:

1. Allocate specific, specialized job duties to each person on your crew, so that each becomes a specialist in one field. For example, a framing crew of two can go from job to job with nothing to do but frame walls and partitions.

2. Develop standard dimensions for such often-used items of material as 2 x 4 studs and sheathing, so that cutting and fitting can be minimized and systematized.

3. Foster a spirit of teamwork among your crew by letting each of them understand your overall methods and goals.

4. Schedule the work of subcontractors so as to minimize their time losses due to poor planning on your part.

5. Plan material needs far enough ahead that sufficient amounts of material of the correct dimensions are on the job site the day they are needed. In most cases, the only way to combat possible deliv-

ery delays is to have material delivered before it is needed.

An Alternative: Components

Components, such as preconstructed roof trusses—as well as precut lumber—decrease construction time. Some precuts and components may be shipped from distant manufacturers; some may be manufactured at your local lumberyard. While components undoubtedly offer a savings in actual construction time, this savings has to be examined in light of the additional original cost. It is doubtful, for example, that your local lumber dealer can precut framing lumber to your specifications any less expensively than one of your carpenters' helpers, using a portable power saw. On the other hand, components such as roof trusses and door and window frames may be constructed more accurately in the lumberyard than your workers could accomplish it on the job site.

Prefabs

The use of prefabricated house sections can decrease your need for a large work force. If you decide to use prefabs extensively or exclusively, the major portion of your work will be in preparing the site, assembling the prefabricated sections, and completing the finish work of the house.

To keep your work crew scheduled efficiently when using prefabricated sections, you will have to devote considerable attention to having building sites ready when the prefabs are delivered. Your crew should have a systematic method of working that will enable them to progress from one site to the other without delays.

Unfinished Houses

Another approach to home building, especially in the lower price range, is to build a house that is completed to a stage at which the owner can take occupancy and do the interior finish work himself, thereby effecting a savings on the total price of the house. This method has the obvious advantage of appealing to a lower-income group of buyers, but has several disadvantages that should be carefully considered:

1. Lending institutions may be reluctant to take mortgages on houses on which there is no assurance that the finished work will be competently done.
2. Houses that are poorly finished may in the long run adversely affect your reputation as a builder.
3. By blatantly appealing to a low-income market, you may foster cut-rate practices that could result in a disastrous competitive situation.

The Future of Construction

Technology promises many new construction materials and techniques for the future. Just how many of these new materials and techniques will stand the test of time is yet to be seen, but it is your job as an independent builder to keep abreast of all new developments in construction. You can do this by joining trade associations, reading trade publications, and maintaining a general alertness concerning the future of building.

9

Failure, Half-Success, and Success

New businesses of all kinds have a high mortality rate in all parts of the United States. Many specific reasons could be given for the failures, aside from the very general reason that a new business is extremely difficult to establish in a competitive field. A few businesses never really fail, but they never quite prosper. And on the other side of the coin, a few businesses succeed. Enough businesses succeed, in fact, to keep alive the American dream of becoming independent with a business of your own.

In this chapter, I will give you a few specific reasons for the failures, half-successes, and successes. As an actual case history of a business that failed, let's consider a real firm, to which I will give a fictitious name, McCandless Builders.

HOW THE McCANDLESS BUILDERS FAILED

Tom McCandless grew up in a Colorado town, the son of an established builder in the area. He followed in his father's footsteps, establishing a moderately successful business base from which he built approximately 125 houses. Then, due to the removal of an industry from the area, Tom's business fell off dramatically. He then decided to move to Oregon, where he had spent parts of two summers on fishing vacations.

Tom's first mistakes in his new Oregon location were to choose a poor site for his first speculative house and to incorporate some design features in the house that had been popular in Colorado but were somewhat "foreign" in Oregon. Fifteen months later, when the house finally sold, Tom's net profit on the venture had dwindled to $400, due to mortgage fees that hadn't been planned for.

Meanwhile, while waiting for his speculative house to be sold, Tom had the misfortune of accepting employment with a cut-rate building firm that eventually fell into disfavor with both the public and the lending institutions of the area. However, Tom did gain some experience in a field of building with which he had little previous contact: home remodeling and repair.

And Then—A Series of Changes

Tom's next job was with a firm that aimed its product to an extremely low-income group, financed with the maximum interest charges that the law would allow. The houses built by this firm were barely up to standards on building codes and built with marginally acceptable materials. Not only was the *modus operandi* of this firm quite similar to that of the cut-rate firm Tom had worked for, but its record for meeting obligations was also poor.

Even though Tom knew the shortcomings of this new employer, when the manager offered him the chance to change his status from employee to subcontractor, he accepted it. According to the agreement between him and the firm, he was to do all the carpentry work on the houses built under the firm's name, for a set price.

To act as subcontractor for this firm, Tom had to hire four carpenters and a working foreman, all of whom furnished their own hand tools, thereby minimizing Tom's need for equipment. Within the next two years, Tom and his men built approximately 100 houses, with Tom assuming the duties of management, including record keeping and the purchasing of materials.

Because the houses were marginally priced, and because Tom's parent firm was often slow and unreliable in paying him, Tom undertook to branch out and work for other firms in the area as a subcontractor. Now he was making the mistake of trying to build a success on the basis of already near-failure, and spreading himself too thin while he did it. By spreading himself so thin, he had less and less time to use good management procedure, including the keeping of records. Then, on the basis of his experience in repair/remodeling, he decided to go into partnership with a salesman for a repair/remodeling firm, George Hanson. His decision was to operate the repair/remodeling business as a sideline. The new firm was to be called the McCandless-Hanson Builders.

Now—Too Many Details

Tom and George's plan was that George, with his selling experience and knowledge of the markets, would oversee the sales of home repair/remodeling jobs, while Tom, with his building experience, would perform the jobs. To this end, Tom and George established an office for the McCandless-Hanson Builders, with Tom providing most of the capital, which consisted mainly of tools, building equipment, and a few items of office equipment. Meanwhile, Tom was actively engaged in his subcontracting jobs for his original and two other parent firms.

The McCandless-Hanson Builders employed salesmen who canvassed the area door-to-door. When one of the salesmen turned up a good prospect for a home repair or remodeling job, George Hanson, an expert "closer," would close the sale and take care of the paperwork, which included financing for the customer through FHA Title I loans. If and when credit was approved, Tom would prepare a plan to be approved by the city and county building departments; when the building permit was issued, Tom would pull a few men off the subcontracting jobs to do the repair/remodeling jobs. By this time, Tom was so diversified in his activities that he had no idea if his men were being scheduled efficiently; he had no idea of the true relationship between his gross income and cost of operating; and he was keeping only incomplete records of purchases.

Meanwhile, Tom's original parent company, for whom he was still acting as subcontractor, was falling further and further behind in payments to him. By his poor record keeping, and by swapping dollars with his other ventures, Tom kept himself practically unaware of the devastating effect on him of the poor payment record of this company.

The Day of Truth

Finally, when Tom had approximately fifteen houses in various stages of completion for the original parent firm, he learned that no more money would be forthcoming from this firm. By this time, he had fallen in arrears on his own payments to materials suppliers. When they pressed him for payment, his obligations became so overwhelming that he filed a voluntary petition in bankruptcy.

In the court proceeding that resulted from Tom's bankruptcy, he was advised to sell his interest in the McCandless-Hanson Builders to his partner. However, since the job of production management had fallen to Tom in this firm, and since he had kept inadequate and incomplete records from the outset, no appreciable assets of the firm could be located. Therefore, from the McCandless-Hanson Builders venture, Tom was left with some unpaid bills as well as poor customer relations that resulted from long delays in completing some remodeling jobs while Tom was involved in his bankruptcy proceedings.

The Lessons to Be Learned

What specific factors caused Tom's failure? To be sure, he would appear to have been the victim of unworthy associates, but he can assume most of the blame for his failure, for the following reasons:

1. Upon moving to a new location (from Colorado to Oregon), he did not analyze the market conditions in his new environment properly.
2. He used poor judgment in taking his first job in the area with a firm that substituted cut-rate building practices for quality.
3. He also used poor judgment in securing his second employment in the area with a firm that catered to a low-income group and operated on a marginal profit basis. He then compounded this mistake by allowing himself to become involved with this same firm as a subcontractor.
4. By taking on more contracting jobs (without severing his relationship with the original firm), and branching out into a partnership venture, he spread himself so thin that he couldn't give adequate supervision to any one of his ventures.
5. Since he kept records in a haphazard manner, he never really understood his financial condition.

After Tom's various enterprises collapsed, he again had to secure employment and he went to work for a general contractor of the area. Before he can ever go back into business for himself, he will have to find some means of getting a reinstatement of his contractor's license, which he lost as a result of his bankruptcy.

THE JONES CASE:
EXPANSION INTO FAILURE

Jones Builders is also a fictitious name, but the case of failure outlined here is factual. Jones Builders was actually Jones Builders, Inc. It began life with a capitalization of $40,000, put up by Jones and two associates. Of these three men, Jones was the experienced craftsman, having been in the building business, both for himself and as a supervisor for various firms, for the past twenty years. The last two of that twenty years had been spent as a general superintendent for one of the largest home development and construction firms in the area, in the production end of the business.

With a good background in building, and with a moderate amount of capital, Jones Builders, Inc., got off to a good start by buying and developing land upon which to build houses in groups of from fifteen to twenty-five. At any given time, the firm would have approximately twenty-five houses in various stages of completion, with the sales of the houses virtually assured. Jones Builders, Inc., met all obligations when due.

The Expansion Syndrome

When the firm was into its second year of operation, Jones suggested to his associates that they begin building houses in groups of 50 to 100. They made this expansion, and sales kept up with production, with profits increasing accordingly. Then, however,

Jones began to pressure his associates for more and more expansion. One of Jones's associates, who had considerable business background, disagreed with Jones, giving as his reason the fact that the firm had insufficient capital to justify further expansion. As a result of the disagreement, Jones's associates left the firm, selling their interests to Jones and his wife, making them the sole owners of Jones Builders, Inc.

Jones's first act of expansion was to form affiliate companies, one to manufacture roof trusses for residential and industrial buildings, and the other to buy and develop land and build speculative houses, operating anywhere in the state that it chose. In effect, the truss-manufacturing company was a captive company, routing most of its production to Jones Builders, Inc. Jones assumed the role of general contractor for the other affiliate firm and was soon heavily involved in various kinds of construction around the state. Within six months, Jones Builders, Inc., with its affiliate companies, had several hundred residential starts in the state, but it was relying heavily on borrowed capital to pay the overhead and day-to-day expenses of the burgeoning enterprises.

The Collapse

When Jones's building empire collapsed, 75 of the 700 houses that he had started were in the process of being sold. The visible reason for the failure of the remaining homes to be sold on schedule was a market that was oversaturated with houses, together with a widespread regional economic slump. By that time,

Jones was used to handling millions of dollars in paper transactions, with no substantial amounts of cash involved. He had built offices for his firm in several parts of the state. But the wave of prosperity that he had been riding ended in chaos when the housing market bottomed out.

By the time Jones fully realized his financial condition, he was operating almost entirely on borrowed money and was also heavily in debt to many of his suppliers and subcontractors. When his creditors began pressing him for payment, he was forced to file for bankruptcy proceedings. Many of his completed homes were sold at auction.

The Lessons to Be Learned

As in the case of Tom McCandless, the reason for Jones's failure seemed, outwardly, to be largely due to unfortunate circumstances. But, as in the case of McCandless, Jones can assume most of the blame for his failure, for the following reasons:

1. Jones's first mistake was in not delegating *business* management duties to his business-wise associate and *production* management duties to himself, and then taking the advice of his associate.

2. Even without business knowledge, Jones should have been knowledgeable enough about the housing market to see that he was working in boom conditions, which could well be followed by a ''bust.''

3. Even if Jones had adequate capital to justify his ex-

pansion, he should not have set up operations over which he could not exert at least occasional direct supervision.

Jones's expanded enterprises involved millions of dollars; however, overexpansion of a building business is possible on a smaller scale. Remember that you must always calculate the additional cost of expansion, in the form of new management labor, new facilities, and additional equipment (as well as the additional interest to be paid on loans secured to finance equipment) against the expected additional gross income that the expansion will bring. There is usually a point beyond which the small business had best not expand without the addition of new operating capital.

NOT A FAILURE—BUT NOT A SUCCESS

A case history of neither a total failure nor a total success is that of Harvey Simonson (also a fictitious name). Harvey discontinued college, where he was majoring in business administration, to work as a carpenter's helper. Within two years this activity had led him into his own business of manufacturing wooden kitchen cabinets, in partnership with a home repair/remodeling salesman. Within another year, he and his partner sold this business and went into the building business, doing both speculative and custom building. The partner brought to the association some money as well as some sales contacts; he took an active role in selling and record keeping but no role in actual construction.

Harvey's partnership firm built homes in the middle-income range, completing eight to ten homes a year at a profit of approximately 15 percent. In a few months, however, the partnership was dissolved because Harvey thought that a sole proprietorship would be more advantageous than a partnership under the circumstances. During the next two years, Harvey built approximately five homes a year, still in the middle-income range, through his sole proprietorship firm. His next step was to incorporate, and with additional operating capital, he increased his production schedule to ten houses a year. Still taking the conservative approach, he built exclusively on a contract basis with the customer, sometimes using the customer's lot, sometimes using a lot that he had purchased out of his earnings. However, as the price of land steadily increased, Harvey became reluctant to invest his own money in land and built exclusively on the customers' lots.

From a Meager Beginning

I should mention here that Harvey's invested capital in the original partnership was quite modest, consisting of a small amount of cash and a minimal amount of equipment. But even at that time, because of labor costs, his overhead was disproportionately large. Despite a small additional capitalization when he incorporated, after ten years of work his assets had increased very little, still consisting of a small amount of operating capital and a moderate amount of tools, along with some building and office equipment (he always maintained his office at his home). The best that could be said for his business during that ten-year period is that it was "fairly steady." But by the eleventh year, business became poor. Then, because he had managed to acquire some land of his own, he decided to switch from custom building to speculative building.

The Reasons for the Change

Because of his conservative business principles, Harvey had spent very little for advertising during his first ten years as a builder. He had been watchful where quality was concerned, with the result that as long as there had been a strong housing market, he had managed to land enough jobs to satisfy his income needs as well as buy some land. When the housing market declined slightly, however, he felt compelled to make the change to speculative building.

And Other Problems

Some of the problems Harvey coped with in the custom building business were probably in fact largely circumstantial. It is inherent in the custom building business that the estimating of jobs is extremely risky in a competitive market. Some of the difficulties of estimating stemmed from a large number of variables—especially in the carpenter work that Harvey specialized in. As another factor, many of the customers provided their own architectural plans, which were often vague and deficient in the specification of material grades. By contrast, the speculative builder, who can build tract homes, is in a much stronger position when it comes to estimating costs.

As a typical example of the kind of problem that can arise in the estimating of a custom-built house, if the customer's plans are vague concerning the quality of roofing to be used, there could be a variable factor of several hundred dollars in the estimating, depending upon the roofing that was finally decided upon. This meant that Harvey would have to hold consultations with the customer, which could involve delay as well as hours of explaining and discussing different material grades.

Harvey got around many of the headaches of estimating by using subcontractors for all but the carpentry work on a house. To arrive at estimates on the material for carpentry, his usual method was to take the blueprints to the local lumberyard, where the manager would estimate the amount and price of the material needed. Concrete, which he purchased from a ready-mix company, was relatively simple to estimate; but labor costs, in a situation in which each house differed from the previous one, could be difficult to estimate. In fact, there were times when his final estimate on a custom job might vary between $1,000 and $1,500 from the actual cost of the job.

To compile a summary of his costs, Harvey used a "Construction Cost Estimate and Lien Release Check Sheet," a form furnished by his Federal Savings and Loan Association. He maintained comprehensive records of his costs from the time he incorporated. If he had been as competent at building as he was with business principles, his business might have prospered.

Using Hindsight to Find the Answers

In analyzing his problems of the past ten years, Harvey decided that he had been working in an inflationary period, when the relationship between the cost of land and the cost of construction had changed in such a manner as to narrow the margin of profit that a builder could make. He compounded his circumstantial problems by taking on varied interests, even taking university classes while a full-time construction foreman did the major part of his direct supervisory work. In spite of our earlier cautionary remarks concerning the diverting of one's attention from a business through other activities, it is not impossible to operate a business while holding down another job or attending school. In Harvey's case, his diversified interests may have been a contributing factor to his being forced out of custom building.

Harvey did keep detailed records of materials used and their costs, the scheduling of labor, and the scheduling of production. He was aware of when materials were ordered, when they were delivered, and when they were installed. He knew, within fairly close limits, when a certain phase of construction on a house should be complete, and he had a good general idea of how long it took to construct a custom-built house of a given square footage.

Harvey, as a careful buyer, had always balanced the

factors of cost, quality, and service from suppliers against one another; since variations in prices were insignificant, he placed more emphasis on quality and service. He occasionally took advantage of discounts for quantity buying, and he always paid his supplier promptly enough to qualify for the 2 percent cash discount.

The Change to Speculative Building

After his marginal venture in custom building, Harvey would have gotten out of the building business except for two facts: (1) most of his work experience was now in the building trades, and (2) most of the capital that he had managed to acquire over the years was now tied up in building lots.

Through good foresight, Harvey's land was located in an area where there was still some demand (though a diminishing demand) for middle-income houses. Also, since he owned the building lots, the relationship between the rising cost of land and the rising cost of construction worked in his favor, to allow him to make as much as 15 percent to 20 percent profit. However, he knew that if he misjudged the housing market and the houses did not sell for a year, the interest payments on the borrowed money that he needed for operating capital could be staggering. Due to inflation, customer financing was more difficult to secure than it had previously been, which resulted in a weakened housing market.

The Reasons for Lack of Success

Just as Jones of Jones Builders, Inc., was a construction man but not a businessman, we could say that Harvey leaned a little too heavily toward an interest in business, at the expense of adequate construction supervision. His conservative approach to business, and particularly his reluctance to advertise, were instrumental in keeping him from a high degree of success.

The Reasons for Not Failing

The characteristics that kept Harvey from totally succeeding also kept him from total failure. His conservatism, his attention to business detail, and, most important, his refusal to attempt expansion with inadequate capital in an uncertain market, kept him alive in the building business. He was astute enough in business to keep his personal expenditures separate from business expenditures, and he met all obligations promptly. Therefore, at the crucial time in his business experience, he was able to make an orderly transition. But we can neither say that Harvey was a success nor call him a failure.

BUILDERS, INC.—SUCCESS ON A SHOESTRING

Builders, Inc. (a fictitious name) was a corporation formed by three construction workers for the purpose of offering trade skills to the industry. Specifically, the firm would draw up contracts with the building firms of the area to subcontract all the masonry and carpentry work on a project. The contract would stipulate a firm price for the labor, with the explicit understanding that Builders, Inc., would not furnish any material.

Builders, Inc., was an association of three extremely competent craftsmen who not only knew the building trade but also knew how to recruit and organize an efficient working crew. To perform each job efficiently, they developed production-line techniques, with each man on the crew specializing in some kind of masonry or carpentry phase of the job. The function of the firm was to build the entire house, starting with the construction of the foundation forms, up to and including the installation of doors, windows, and finish trim in the completed house. Because of the "specialist" concept, each man knew at all times exactly what he was supposed to do and could keep himself busy at all times. Therefore, each job was completed in the shortest possible time.

The success story of Builders, Inc., was based on the premise of "seeing a need and filling it." It combined the elements of craftsmanship, a well-developed plan of operation, and a system of bidding that allowed the company to work on a small margin of profit. Since it was required to furnish no material, it could operate with minimal capital.

The growth of Builders, Inc., was dramatic; during four years, the firm not only provided a living for its associates but increased its capitalization from $3,000 to a net worth of $135,000. We should point out, however, that the three partners drew only wages from the firm during that four years and plowed all the remaining profits back into the business.

A SUCCESS BASED ON AMBITION, ENERGY, AND ORGANIZATIONAL ABILITY

Jerry Almquist (a fictitious name) also started on a moderate amount of capital, and he did it while holding a full-time job as an instructor in the business department of his local community college. Jerry had been on speaking terms with building tradesmen for most of his life, having virtually grown up in his father's lumberyard. His first venture into the building business was during his first summer vacation from his teaching job. He bought a building site, and, recognizing his own inexperience in building, hired a carpenter to act as a working boss on the construction of a house. He worked with the carpenter as a helper. Before his fall term started, the house was complete, and he realized a fair profit from its sale.

The success of his first project hooked Jerry on the idea of building, but since he enjoyed his teaching job, he decided to try building as a sideline activity. Having made a firm friend of his carpenter on this first job, and having accumulated extra capital for operating cash, he retained the carpenter on a full-time basis as a foreman to recruit a crew and oversee all construction. The crew was kept small, since all work but the basic carpentry was subcontracted.

Now, with enough capital to build more houses, a strong housing market, competent employees, and the independence and flexibility that his full-time job gave him, Jerry was in a strong business position. Because of his education and his liking of paperwork, he kept excellent records on all phases of his business. Having grown up in the area where he kept his operations centered, always in contact with the construction business, he had a good grasp of land values and housing market conditions. He understood the economic factors of the area and knew the style and price range of houses that would sell in certain locations.

A Conservative Approach

Because Jerry depended heavily upon the skills of his workmen, he also expected them to furnish their own carpentry tools. He avoided the cost of specialized, expensive equipment by using his local tool-rental service extensively, and he avoided the cost of a pickup truck by compensating his foreman for the use of his pickup. Thus, he kept his equipment inventory small and limited, thereby having available capital for land purchases and building materials.

From the outset, Jerry's building business showed a fair profit. Enough profit, in fact, to have justified his leaving the teaching position to build on a full-time basis. But his teacher's salary allowed him to return profits to the business, which could thereby establish a base of security by building an occasional rental house and by assuming some second mortgages on his speculative houses. Had he quit his teaching job, on the other hand, his living expenses would have consumed the profits from the business in these early years.

Despite this seemingly ultraconservative approach to business, Jerry's long-range plans called for expansion. To this end, he kept his eye constantly on his growing capital and on the housing market and general economic conditions of the area.

The "Break"

It is axiomatic that everyone gets a "lucky break" at some time in life, an opportunity that may be a giant step towards a goal—if the opportunity can be used intelligently. Jerry's break was in the form of a contract to custom build a commercial building: One of the local service organizations, of which Jerry was a member, wanted him to put up a new building for its meetings and social activities.

This commercial job presented some new problems to Jerry, inasmuch as he had been building only residences. However, with an adequate reservoir of operating capital and a work crew that was willing to adapt its basic skills to this new construction challenge, Jerry was able to take on the job.

Fortunately, when a building slump came, Jerry's crew was kept busy on the construction of the new lodge building. By the time the building was completed, Jerry was able to make the adjustments necessary to keep him in home building. One of the factors that worked in his favor was that he was holding land that had been rapidly appreciating in value. And, of course, he always had the independence of his salary.

An Uncomplicated Operating Format

Jerry never tried to expand his operations far from his own home; so he could find time for direct supervision of his building activities. He lived in an area that had been largely agricultural but was gradually changing to suburban, with the result that building lots were turning up in the form of small acreages, usually as a result of the expansion of utilities into these rural areas. To keep abreast of these developments, Jerry attended the meetings of county and city planning commissions, he talked with people, and he combed the classified ad section of his local newspaper.

Jerry stuck with just a few basic home designs, thereby simplifying the chore of keeping accurate cost records on construction. While he depended heavily upon his foreman to supervise the actual construction, Jerry himself compiled these cost records. When a house was completed, he immediately knew exactly what sale price would bring the amount of profit that he required. When a house was ready for sale, he simply placed an advertisement in the real estate section of the classified ads and put a "For Sale" sign in front of the house. By his sixth year of operation he had established a good reputation as a builder.

The Value of Friendships

Because Jerry had grown up in a business-oriented atmosphere, he knew the value of friendships and social contacts. He knew the subcontractors of the area so well that he could bypass the usual bidding procedure and simply work with one whom he knew and trusted. This put his relationship with subcontractors on a friendly basis, in which both understood and appreciated the business problems of the other. Thus, if a subcontractor made an estimate that ultimately proved to be too low, Jerry would adjust the terms of the contract to allow the subcontractor to make his normal profit. If, on the other hand, the subcontractor estimated a job too high, he would adjust the final price to Jerry's satisfaction.

Jerry also maintained a good relationship with his wife, who helped him with his bookkeeping; with his father, who, though retired, still had important business contacts in town; with general contractors, who helped him keep abreast of new developments in the trade; with other businessmen of the area, who helped keep him informed about economic trends; and with his own working crew, whom he considered competent and reliable. To keep skilled, competent workmen, he always endeavored to keep enough projects going to retain full-time employees, for whom he provided paid vacations, payment into a pension fund, and other benefits. He took an active interest in civic affairs through both his lodge and individual activities. He never shied from favorable publicity.

A Minimal Material Inventory

Contrary to what some builders consider to be good buying methods, Jerry never tried to get price breaks through quantity buying, but he did get good service from suppliers, along with the normal discount for cash buying. Because he got prompt delivery he could carry a minimal inventory, thereby eliminating the need for storage facilities and the extensive book-keeping that goes with a perpetual inventory. To defend himself against increases in material prices, he charged all purchased materials against specific houses, which he sold within a reasonable time at a profit determined by construction costs. His only problem with this method of materials purchasing was to always be sure that suppliers could fill his needs immediately as needed. However, since he planned production carefully and never used unusual materials, he was never forced into long delays while waiting for materials.

Quick Turnover

I have already pointed out that Jerry thoroughly understood the housing market of his area. Therefore, his houses seldom stood for any appreciable length of time after being built. In most cases, houses were sold virtually as fast as they were built, with the time range of sales being from about one month before a house was completed to about one month after completion. This fast pace of sales allowed him to pick and choose among his customers, thereby minimizing his risks in taking second mortgages. And, by making sales while in the process of building other houses, he always had available cash with which to meet obligations.

The favorable market conditions in which Jerry worked also kept his sales-related expenses to a minimum, since he had no broker's commission to pay. Both he and his wife came to understand the paperwork involved in sales and handled all the details of each sale themselves. His only expense in selling—aside from the normal fees for clearing title, etc.—was in the few classified ads that he ran in his local newspaper.

Finally—Assets That Exceed Liabilities

At the end of the first six years of operation, Jerry's financial balance sheet showed assets far in excess of his current liabilities. At this point, if he wished, he was in a strong position to borrow money for expansion.

The Reasons for Success

It would be a temptation to believe that Jerry's success was due primarily to keeping his job and operating his business as a sideline. However, many who have tried to "moonlight" while operating a building business have either failed or met with little success. Some of the reasons for Jerry's success were:

1. A solid background in a construction-related business.
2. Direct supervision of all the costing analyses of building.
3. An ability to take advantage of an opportunity when it came along.
4. College-level business education and attention to the record-keeping aspects of the business.

5. A knowledge of economic conditions and the local housing market, together with willingness not to deviate from locally accepted housing styles and prices.
6. Intelligent purchasing of land for building sites.
7. A reluctance to invest heavily in materials and equipment, which left Jerry with operating cash with which to buy needed materials—as well as land, when available—for cash.
8. Intelligent use of workmen's skills.

Finally, Jerry Almquist was lucky to be working in a housing market that was fairly strong, except for the temporarily depressed period when he built the lodge building. However, most successful businessmen do have the uncanny ability to be "doing the right thing, in the right place, at the right time."

A SUCCESS BASED ON MANAGERIAL SKILL

For a different kind of success story, we will turn to Jim Harriman (a fictitious name). Harriman didn't decide to go into the building business for himself until he was well past middle age. At that point, he had considerable background in construction as well as some education in engineering and architecture (but no college degree). He also had some sales experience.

To achieve a business format that Harriman believed would take him toward his business goals, he formed a family corporation; he and his wife held thirty shares each in the corporation, and his mother held fifteen shares. Three enterprises were incorporated separately: One was the Harriman Building Company; one was LandFinders, Inc.; and one was HomeBuilders, Inc. The initial aim of the Harriman Building Company was to engage in carpentry subcontracting, speculative home building, and general construction on a contract basis. LandFinders, Inc., was formed solely to search out, purchase, and develop undeveloped acreages for resale. Home-Builders, Inc., was formed to build low-priced tract homes in another region but in the same state. The name given to the aggregate enterprises was the Harriman Building Company, Inc.

A Slow Beginning

The growth of the Harriman Building Company, Inc., was by no means phenomenal and not without its early problems. Its first activity, which was in the repair/remodeling field, almost failed. The reason for this lack of success was not readily apparent, although it can probably be linked to two factors: (1) Harriman was reluctant to use operating capital for advertising and depended primarily upon word-of-mouth publicity, and (2) although he was experienced in many phases of building and construction, he was not well grounded in the careful estimating required in repair/remodeling.

Now Harriman decided to specialize in carpentry subcontracting, which seemed to offer a more secure base for his business operations. At the outset of this new activity, he was able to draw up contracts with approximately twenty building firms of various sizes, all of whom were building speculative houses in groups of from three to twenty on their various lots. To cover this much ground, he had to increase his full-time work crew from four to fifteen employees, with as many as twenty-five to thirty workmen being used at the height of the building season. In this particular area, this was the beginning of an era when general contractors relied heavily on subcontractors for the basic carpentry work on houses, which is the service that Harriman undertook to provide.

And Then—Diversification

Since most of his working experience had been in supervising field crews, Harriman was at home in his new activity. When he saw the potential that new home construction offered the general contractor, he sought out some contracts for home and small commercial projects. When this activity was established on a profitable basis, he used available operating capital to branch out into the speculative building market, which had the incidental effect of providing a means to keep his crews busy between contract jobs.

Despite this diversification, the growth of Harriman's enterprises was not dramatic, and in the fifth year of operation, the company had about 40 homes in various stages of completion, built on land acquired through LandFinders, Inc. In the tenth year of operation, it was decided that the Harriman Building Company would return to subcontracting and general contracting and turn its speculative building over to its related enterprise, HomeBuilders, Inc. The short-range production goal for HomeBuilders, Inc. was 300 homes within the next two years.

The Intelligent Use of Credit as a Source of Operating Capital

From the very beginning, Harriman's investment in Harriman Building was not large. He depended heavily on supplier credit as well as bank loans to pay those bills that were due before he received payment for a completed contract. While this method may not work for everyone, he had two advantageous conditions working for him: (1) he was thought of by the lending institutions of his area as a competent manager, and (2) he was operating in a time when building loans were relatively easy to obtain.

In its eleventh year of operation, the Harriman Building Company owned outright several vehicles as well as a moderate number of power tools. The company kept only a minimal amount of materials and supplies on hand, preferring instead to rely upon its excellent relationships with suppliers to provide materials and supplies when needed. The company was heavily bulwarked with both casualty and liability insurance, which is a necessity in the construction business. And to be assured that the company would survive in case of his untimely death, Harriman had purchased a $100,000 term life insurance policy, designating his associates as beneficiaries.

Adjusting to Capital Shortages

There were times when the size of a speculative

building project would cause the problem of deficient operating capital. For example, a fifty-home project might require a large amount of capital to be expended before building could commence. At such a time, the availability of borrowed capital would depend upon the current strength of the housing market, which was not always without its problems. To overcome such problems, Harriman decided that he could either build houses in smaller groups, thereby minimizing his capital needs, or build in larger groups and develop a method of selling that would provide him with more liquid funds. He decided to build in smaller groups.

Direct Supervision

Despite the fact that Harriman was operating a corporate entity, he always endeavored to give direct supervision to his various activities whenever possible. In the matter of cost analyses, for example, he himself reduced all the cost factors involved in building a house to a worksheet, on which he listed all the various phases of carpentry, masonry, subcontractors' costs, and so on. The worksheet provided information regarding the workmen and man-hours involved in each specific phase of the building of a specific house, as well as all materials used, with the cost of the materials noted.

In the matter of estimating, an extremely simplified system was developed for tract houses. Because of careful analysis of all the costs involved in construction, Harriman was able to make estimates that were based simply on the square footage of the house. But even with this method, cost analyses were continued in order to perfect the system and provide a basis for future estimating.

The cost analysis for building a house was quite easily converted into a selling price. This does not mean, however, that each successive house of the same footage would sell for an identical price, since the changing costs of labor and material, during a period of continuing but erratic inflation, always had to be considered. Harriman's system of estimating was accepted by suppliers, who could quickly use his blueprints to give him estimates of material costs for each new job. Other builders of the area came to recognize and use this method of estimating. However, any builder attempting to adapt to a system developed by someone else must remember that he must include figures derived from his own cost analyses, since certain cost factors are sure to differ between builders. Harriman also worked continuously to improve construction methods, so that all the jobs could be done quickly and efficiently.

Success of the Related Enterprises

The success of Harriman's related enterprises—LandFinders, Inc., and HomeBuilders, Inc.—played a large part in the overall success of the corporation. LandFinders, Inc., which was managed by an associate of Harriman's who had considerable experience in buying, developing, and selling land, listed company assets of approximately $250,000 in the eleventh year of operation. Aside from good managerial supervision, the success of LandFinders, Inc., could be attributed to the facts that (1) the state had large undeveloped areas lying close to the cities, which could usually be bought quite cheaply; and (2) these acreages could only be developed successfully by fairly large operators, because the problems of development included road building, well drilling, and the installation of utilities. The immigration of city dwellers to these newly developed outlying areas was encouraged by a general longing of many people to get away from the pollution and noise of the city.

HomeBuilders, Inc., was given a big boost in its eleventh year of operation when the head of that enterprise was able to obtain a large loan from a friend on favorable terms. With this additional capital, HomeBuilders, Inc., bought lots from Land Finders, Inc. These lots were located in one of the choicer sections of the region. With the help of the choice lots and additional capital, HomeBuilders was in a position to aim for the middle-income housing market, which would bring a considerably better return for each dollar invested in labor and material than would that same dollar invested in labor and material for the low-income housing market.

Reasons for Success

The most outstanding and relevant reasons for Harriman's success in his related enterprises were his technical competence and good managerial ability. Also, he chose associates who were competent and knowledgeable in the construction and land-development business. He operated in economic conditions favorable to the housing market, which made both operating capital and customer financing relatively easy to obtain. Finally, despite the expansiveness of his enterprises, he usually took a conservative approach to solving business problems, avoiding the temptation to spend large sums of money on highly speculative projects.

10

Looking Ahead

The owner-manager of a building business (or any other business) who doesn't acknowledge the need for planning will probably ''wing it'' right into a business failure. On certain levels of operation, this need for planning becomes quite obvious. For example, it is costly to have a carpenter and carpenter's helper forced into idleness while waiting for the subcontractor who won't arrive on time because the manager of the business didn't make plans properly.

The need for short-range planning, therefore, is so obvious that the point hardly needs belaboring. But not so obvious is the need for moderate- and long-range planning. You must be thinking 90 days ahead, for instance, to the season when inclement weather has its traditional effect on housing starts; will you have sufficient work at that time to keep your full-time workers productively employed? What about 120 days from now, when the expansion of utilities into outlying areas should dramatically increase housing starts? Will you have sufficient operating capital (or a loan source) with which to take advantage of this new opportunity?

Taken in the larger scheme of your operation, these short-range and moderate-range plans can be thought of as subgoals, much as the stratagems in a football game are subgoals that take the team on to its end goal. The end goal itself, in the case of the building business, can be thought of in terms of five, ten, or fifteen years from now. What would happen to your business if, for example, (1) the building industry in general were to change dramatically, with new, synthetic materials used in place of traditional wood and radically different requirements for conserving energy; (2) your son—or trusted employee—whom you are priming for a top managerial position, decides to quit you and go to work elsewhere; or (3) because of an increasingly intense competitive situation, you are forced to choose between expansion or failure.

We'll explore the ways in which the resourceful manager plans for such contingencies, but before we do, I must inject a cautionary note about *overplanning*. A rigid, unalterable plan of operation forces a business into a restricted position, making it extremely difficult to cope with conditions that are changed continually by external and unforeseeable circumstances. For example, the manager who adopts a conservative approach to business may be using the right general method when the business is launched, but if he refuses to take expansion steps when they are justified, simply because such steps weren't included in the plans, he will find himself repeating one of the failure or half-success stories that you read in the previous chapter. For a plan to be viable, it must be flexible enough to allow for a *change in plans* if it becomes necessary.

CHANGES IN THE INDUSTRY

To say that the future of your business will be influenced by changes in the building industry is an understatement. Without the aid of a crystal ball, we know that the industry is virtually at the threshold of an age when the need to conserve energy is going to dictate building methods. Will it cause a dramatic change in the kinds of material that you will be using? Maybe—and maybe not. But, whatever happens, you should keep yourself aware of the coming trends and be prepared to cope with them.

Some authorities say that we are depleting our timber resources; other authorities deny this. If such a possibility does indeed exist, it could possibly lead to the extensive use of synthetic materials. How would such a change affect you, as a custom or speculative builder?

What would happen if runaway inflation were to combine with a shortage of those wood products that are available for houses that are built with *traditional materials,* by *traditional methods?* The result could well be a heightening of a trend that has already begun: the manufacture of components in the factory, where synthetic products, together with mass-production methods, can cut costs.

Factory-made components, along with the more extensive use of synthetics, could work to reduce the cost of housing and could make dramatic changes in the activities of the average builder. Your problems then might center more around merchandising and selling and less around the technical aspects of building a house. With more time for selling and non-construction-related activities, the builder of tomorrow will probably be branching out into such activities as land development.

Once the traditional mold in home building is broken (if it ever is), the resourceful builder who has stayed abreast of the market demands may be in a stronger and more versatile position than ever before. For example, if and when houses come to look more and more like something that comes off an assembly line, the demand for the custom-built house, built to the customer's own taste, could well comprise an important segment of the housing market.

Any changes that might occur in housing styles and construction methods also imply a changing U.S. economy. Will it be an economy more—or less—oriented to providing housing for low-income groups? Is there a possibility that the government will go further than it already has in helping certain income groups to obtain housing? Will local governments continue the trend that has begun, of offering incentives, in the forms of rebates, for the weatherizing of homes? All this is pure speculation, of course, but we know that the builder who keeps himself informed and involved in new methods of housing financing will clearly have the advantage in the housing market of tomorrow.

PLANNING FOR FUTURE MANAGEMENT

If you are success oriented from the beginning, you will hire workers, or choose associates, with an eye to how they can be trained as key personnel in your growing business. As you select people with this in mind, you will be thinking about both the *technical* aspects and the *business* aspects of your operation.

The Technical Aspects

When you hire a person whom you hope to train to take over many of the technical details of your work, what characteristics do you look for? The person should be a competent craftsman, of course. And regardless of chronological age, the employee should have mature judgment. However, if this person is to develop into the sort of individual that you need, more than craftsmanship is needed. One requirement is a willingness to listen and learn and to continue learning. A second requirement is self-motivation, a willingness to grasp a situation and go ahead when there is no one around to give orders. The employee should have the potential to be a manager, which implies much more than a knowledge of construction; it implies also an innate ability to get along with (but not be pushed around by) people. These people would be the crew to be supervised; the subcontractors with whom to work; suppliers from whom to buy materials; the customers who buy your houses; and the surveyor, the county engineer, the city manager, the building inspector, the wiring inspector, the plumbing inspector—and even the county tax assessor who comes to assess the value of your house while it's still under construction.

The person you choose who meets all—or most—of these qualifications should have one additional important quality: enough security in your firm so as not to be afraid, in turn, to train a subordinate to whom to delegate authority in case the need should arise. Being able to recognize abilities in others and help them into key positions in the company is a related skill. In this manner, you will be able to build a management team that can handle your business without your constant supervision.

The Business Aspects

The other half of your total business is the one that involves the paperwork and record keeping, which keeps its finger always on the financial pulse of your operation. We have already discussed this aspect in some detail. What kind of person do you choose to help you manage it?

First, the person whom you hope to train to manage your office work should be as oriented toward that work as your construction manager is toward technical skills. Together with a high degree of interest in record keeping, letter writing, filing, ordering, and taking phone calls, your office manager needs a good background in the form of education or experience. This means, unfortunately, that the relative who envisions this job as a pleasant way to pass the day may not have the qualifications, or the potential, for managerial duties.

Second, your potential office manager should have the same innate ability to train and handle people as does your construction manager, if and when your business gets large enough to justify additional office help. He or she should understand and agree with your business goals, know how to respond to customer complaints, understand your policies concerning customer credit, know your methods of dealing with salespeople, and be able to convey your ideas to these people just as you yourself would.

Don't be discouraged if the first persons you hire don't fulfill all your expectations. It takes time to build the right kind of work force. When you refill vacancies, try to choose from qualified persons who have a background in the skills you require and a good employment record. Finally, you will be able to build a management team that can handle your business without your constant attention and supervision. Then, and only then, you can say that you have built yourself a business and not simply bought yourself a job.

CAPITAL FOR THE FUTURE

The small entrepreneur in most lines of work is in a difficult situation in the American business community of today. This is nowhere more true than in the building business. If you're like most small-business owners, you'll find it difficult to *begin small* and *grow large* without a source of *growth capital*. In chapter 9, I described a case history in which a builder could plow profits back into his business because the salary from his full-time position as a teacher provided him with a living. In another case, the partners were able to plow profits back into the business because they sold only their skills, with a minimal outlay for equipment and materials. But the average builder who attempts to nurture a business from small beginnings is faced with a myriad of expenses that tend to restrict capital growth.

One builder summed this problem up when he said, ''It's hard to start a small business and stay small. There is a time when you're faced with the choice—either expand or get out of business. Well, you might be able to operate as a one-man business and make it. The only other alternative we've got now is to aim for volume and go for expansion. But it takes capital to do this.''

When you've reached this crucial point, where will the capital for expansion come from? If you've planned ahead, it could come from a variety of sources—for example, (1) a partner you could take into the business, (2) loans, (3) credit, (4) capitalization through incorporation.

The Partnership

A partnership may bring new money to your enterprise, but you should discuss all the advantages and disadvantages of this kind of business organization with your lawyer.

Loans

In the early stages of your business, while you are still operating on a relatively small scale, endeavor to keep yourself in sound financial condition through good management and by operating within your financial means. This might provide you with a financial statement of sufficient strength to attract loan capital when the crucial time comes for expansion.

Credit

Intelligently used credit is an alternate source of operating capital. It can provide you with a means of moderate and justifiable expansion, in the form of material for new construction starts, and new equipment with which to broaden the scope of your operations. Suppliers who extend credit, however, do not investigate your financial strength as thoroughly as does a loan officer of a bank, which places considerable responsibility on you to use restraint in credit buying. You can plan for future operating capital in the form of credit by always meeting your obligations promptly. This means that you must at all times have a thorough understanding of your current financial strength, as well as the assured income potential of your business. Do not use credit as a means to speculate or to meet your day-by-day living expenses; do use it as a means to attract new business and increase your earning potential.

The Corporation

At this point, you might pose the question, "Rather than planning for incorporation in the future, why not incorporate when the business is launched?" If you understand the advantages and disadvantages of a corporation and know that incorporation would be advantageous in your particular situation, and if you can generate interest in the minds of potential stockholders, it may be feasible to incorporate when the business is launched. But if you would prefer to launch the business as a single proprietorship, then future incorporation, after you have tested your building and managerial competence, may be a part of your long-range plans. You would plan for this contingency by keeping your firm financially solvent so that you can attract the confidence of stockholders at the crucial time.

While we often think of corporations as consisting of many stockholders in the general public, a close-knit corporation made up of family members or business associates is one of the more common legal structures for a building business in most states.

The Procedures and Requirements for Incorporating

The procedures and requirements for incorporation are dictated by each state and therefore vary from one state to the other. As a generalized overview of these requirements, I offer the following information, relevant to Oregon. In Oregon the basic requirements are one or more natural persons at the age of twenty-one years or more, $1,000 or equivalent property value as a basis for stock issuance, delivery of articles of incorporation to the corporate commissioner, and a payment of the required fee. Three directors are required, none of whom need to be stockholders or residents of Oregon.

Fees and Expenses of Incorporating. In no case would I recommend that you try to incorporate without the services of a competent lawyer and tax consultant. Therefore, the first major expense incurred in incorporation will be lawyer's fees. Still using Oregon rulings as a general guideline, the Oregon Bar Association recommends a minimum fee for these legal services. To this fee you can also add an accountant's fee. Oregon requires an initial *incorporating* fee, which must be paid at the filing of the articles of incorporation. Additionally, you must pay a prorated *license fee* for the remainder of the year in which you are incorporating; thereafter, an annual license fee must be paid. Both the incorporating fee and license fee are based upon the value of the *authorized* capital stock.

Structure of the Corporation. A corporation consists of three distinct groups: the stockholders, the directors, and the officers. Generally speaking, even though each of these groups may consist of the same persons, there is a definite division of the rights, duties, and responsibilities that accrue to each group.

The Characteristics of a Corporation. Perhaps the outstanding characteristic of the corporation is that it is a legal entity and as such has many—but not all—of the rights of natural persons. It cannot establish an agent or office, or conduct business, in another state, without the authorization of that state. The corporation can live forever, if its charter so provides and certain state requirements are met.

As a legal entity, the corporation is subject to some statutes and regulations that do not apply to proprietorships and partnerships. Also, since owners might not be managers, and vice versa, the operation of a corporation may be quite different from that of a proprietorship or partnership.

Advantages of the Corporation over a Proprietorship or Partnership.   One of the most obvious advantages of the corporation over either of the other two forms is that additional capital can be attracted into the business from interested persons, without those persons participating directly in the making of policies or business decisions. But this advantage is outweighed by several others.

Generally speaking (but check the rulings in your own state), a business may be owned entirely by the corporation, or the corporation may own only such items as vehicles, buildings, or equipment. This is called divisibility of ownership, and through it, a great deal of flexibility in the ownership of the assets of a corporation can be achieved. Another advantage of the corporation is that it does not disintegrate with the death or withdrawal of the major stockholder. Technically, the business can continue without disruption, under the direction of the remaining stockholders, directors, and officers. By contrast, the single proprietorship or partnership business is technically dissolved upon the death or withdrawal of the proprietor or partner, and it must then be reorganized. The business can become disrupted during this transition period.

Through the use of stock purchase agreements, provisions can be made so that any stock offered for sale will be offered first, in some specified manner, to existing stockholders or to the corporation. This has the important advantage of giving surviving stockholders the assurance that there will be continuity of ownership and management, and that stock will not go to disinterested or dissenting stockholders. Such a stock purchase and transfer agreement, together with the stipulation that the corporation can "live forever," are important considerations in establishing an entity that will have continuity.

In a previous section, I mentioned the fact that the corporation structure offers the advantage of limited liability in case of court judgments arising out of lawsuits. In the single proprietorship or partnership, an individual partner's or the proprietor's *personal assets* are subject to claims, or legal judgments, that might be brought against the business. A corporation, being a legal entity, is responsible for contracts and liabilities in its own name, but the personal assets of its members are excluded from such liability. Likewise, the corporation is not liable for personal acts or obligations of its stockholders or employees outside the scope of their corporate activities.

Many persons unfamiliar with corporations believe that the corporation is formed primarily as a tax shelter. While this is not entirely true, the intelligent distribution of income within a corporation does offer some tax advantages. This income distribution can be effected in one of several ways. For example, income can be kept within the corporation, as retained earnings for debt repayment and/or reinvestment. Or funds can be distributed to the corporation employees as salaries, wages, fringe benefits, or to the shareholders as dividends. The manner in which the corporate income is distributed, as a means of getting optimum tax advantages, depends upon the income of the corporation. While this is not a matter that can be completely understood without the help of a tax accountant who will analyze the business situation in accordance with current tax rulings, it derives from the facts that taxation on corporation income, like that on personal income, is graduated in several steps, and that various corporate expenses, including wages and fringe benefits but not dividends, are paid *before* federal taxes are calculated.

Under certain conditions, a corporation may qualify for a "not taxed" status, thereby allowing its stockholders to personally declare its tax losses—and taxable income. However, when this status is taken, the shareholders may have to pay a tax that is disproportionate to their real earnings from the corporation. In any case, before you decide to incorporate, you should carefully consider corporate taxation as it compares with single proprietorship and partnership taxation. Generally speaking, the corporation structure does offer a certain amount of flexibility in the matter of taxation, within certain income brackets.

Another advantage to the corporation is the possibility of establishing tax deductible profit-sharing and pension plans. Also, up to certain limits, the group life insurance premium paid by the employer is excluded from the taxable income of the employee. And, although single proprietorships and partnerships (as well as individuals) can currently take advantage of tax-deferred annuities, the corporation may still gain some tax shelter advantages in this area that are not available to single proprietorships, partners, or individuals.

For reasons that I won't elaborate on here, the corporation also offers considerable flexibility in operational methods that is not available to single proprietors and partnerships. Stockholders can pool, not only their cash, but also their property, equipment, and other resources. This may mean that, if you have operated your business competently as a single proprietorship, you can attract capital for expansion through incorporation. From the beginning, the idea of eventual incorporation could be a part of your long-range planning.

A METHOD OF PLANNING

Earlier in this chapter, I likened the planning of business objectives to the planning of plays in a football game. To carry this analogy further, I could say that the end goal of your business, which is financial solvency within the framework of a business, is analogous to the end goal of the football game, which is to carry the ball across the end line more often than the opposing team does. And, just as the coach and team captain plan to achieve this victory through a series of maneuvers and stratagems called plays, you will achieve your end goal by planning a series of short-range objectives, which could be called subgoals.

The other "team," of course, comprises your competitors; and while your total success doesn't depend upon their total failure, it can be said as a generality that you will be successful to about the same degree that your competitors are unsuccessful. In business terms, this means that some new businesses fail; some succeed.

I can go further with the analogy by saying that the shrewd coach and team captain know that they must depend heavily upon the rest of the team for victory. I have already touched upon the ways that you can foster managerial ability within your organization, so that it will be a strong organization, one that can function competently, even when you are not present to give it direct supervision.

Other than building a solid organization, what are some of the subgoals that might take you forward to your end goal of success in the building business? The following are a few suggested subgoals:

1. From the beginning, even as a one-person firm, establish a reputation among your customers as a reliable, competent, and honest businessperson. Work at this constantly, even though it may cause you occasional inconvenience; the long-range benefits will far outweigh any short-range losses.

2. If you begin as a custom builder or repair/remodeling builder, with a subgoal of becoming a speculative builder, use your profits to buy well-located land as an investment for the future. You may find it feasible to set up an office on your land. Normally, money invested in land appreci-

ates faster than money in a savings account. And you can use the land as (1) collateral for a loan, (2) capital to form a corporation, or (3) building sites.

3. Work to establish a reputation among your peers for meeting all payments and obligations on time. This necessitates the careful use of credit buying, which can work to broaden your base of operations.

4. If one of your subgoals is incorporation, you may wish to reserve a corporation name, which will be exclusively yours. In some states, a name may be reserved prior to incorporation and renewed year to year by making application and paying a nominal fee. If you build your reputation on the name, it can have valuable prestige or advertising value. The name cannot be the same or similar to the name of any existing corporation in your state. Consult with your lawyer for further rulings.

5. At some point in your growth, you may want to broaden your financial base by becoming a franchised dealer for some building product. However, avoid making a large time commitment, which would have to be taken from your primary activities.

6. At some point in your growth, you may wish to invest in a piece of major equipment that will provide a service for which there is a need in your community. Aside from increasing your earnings potential and providing future loan collateral, equipment may also provide a form of

capitalization if one of your subgoals is incorporation.

7. To become more fully self-sufficient in your business, you may wish to gain knowledge of some related activity, such as the use of the surveyor's transit, blueprint drawing, or business mathematics.

8. You may wish to become involved in civic affairs on either a community or county level. This could not only increase your business prestige in the community but also give you invaluable inside information regarding city and county planning as it relates to residential and commercial construction.

9. You may wish to broaden your financial base by building rental housing during a slack time in custom or speculative building.

10. You may wish to reinforce your sales effort in speculative building with a sustained advertising program. To do this, you will have to establish a time schedule for the appearance of display ads and classified ads and for the distribution of brochures that correlate with your building schedule.

The foregoing are only a few of the subgoals, or business objectives, that you may want to include in your plans for the next five years. Such commitments should be flexible, however, so as to allow for orderly changes in case of housing market slumps or other unforeseen financial problems.

What do you do when you find that you have created an entity, staffed with competent managerial personnel, that will practically operate itself without your attention? If this ideal condition should ever arrive, you will have many choices. You can limit your duties to the exclusively managerial; you can think about the prospects for further expansion; or you may think about semiretirement, while your business continues to earn money for you.

11

Developing Land

If you are a speculative builder, land development will at some point in your business growth become a necessary—if costly—activity. The fact that land continues to appreciate in value at about the same rate that inflation invades a bank account is at once a sorrow and a joy. The initial cost of land is high—it may even seem exorbitantly so to the manager of a newly launched small building business; but, as we have already pointed out, money invested in land tends to appreciate faster than money left in a bank account. And, more important, the acquisition of land offers a means of growth for the speculative builder.

HOW AND WHERE TO ACQUIRE LAND

The three basic ways to acquire land for future development are (1) buying either undeveloped acreages or developed sites with the profits from your business, (2) forming a partnership with an individual or company that can bring undeveloped or developed land into the business as a capital contribution, and (3) incorporating your business, seeking out stockholders who can bring land into the business as a capital contribution.

Land should ideally be acquired in areas where there is some current building activity or some other form of assurance that buyers can be attracted there. If you buy developed sites from a land developer, he will probably have found that it is easier to sell a large tract if he allows several builders to operate simultaneously. Normally, the advantages of being involved in a large building project, which attracts interest from prospective buyers, outweigh the disadvantages of competition. You, the small builder, may in fact make the competitive aspects work in your favor by building houses of better quality or more attractive appearance than those of your competitors.

Don't buy either land or developed sites simply because they are available. Study the marketing potential of the area with care; if your study shows that the area has certain undesirable features—such as poor soil characteristics or poor accessibility to commuters' routes—you should probably decide against it.

Other factors to consider in the acquisition of land may be unique to your own plan of operation. For example, you may find that it is more profitable to build houses for the middle-income market than for the low-income market, and this would preclude the use of land in an area where low-income housing predominates. Or you may have detected a trend of buyers away from certain areas, toward other areas. Or you may have reason to believe that an undesirable element will be introduced to an area in the future, which would adversely affect the sales of houses in that area.

It may seem logical to assume that, if other developers and builders are flocking to an area, it must be problem free. However, you shouldn't rely too heavily on the judgment of others in making your own business decisions. Sometimes, for instance, the very fact that an area is burgeoning with newly built houses can create problems. There may not be enough water for everyone. Septic system problems can and do arise in a heavily overbuilt area. Yet, some construction companies will continue to build there. On a more abstract level, certain areas develop unsavory "personalities" that cause the buying public to avoid them. If you are working out of a community where you have lived for a number of years, you will be aware of these kinds of problems. If you are new to a community, investigate all land-buying opportunities thoroughly before making the decision to buy.

DEVELOPING ACREAGES AND UNDEVELOPED LAND

The possibilities for developing acreages or otherwise undeveloped land are limited only to the amount of capital that you have to invest in such an enterprise. You will be faced with new problems, have new challenges to meet and new things to learn.

You may have to buy new equipment or let subcontracts to firms that can build streets and install utilities. A new advertising campaign may have to be planned to attract customers to your newly developed sites as building progresses.

If you have enough capital to meet all the demands of a land-development enterprise, developing your own building sites can bring some advantages. However, aside from the basic considerations that we have discussed, you must take the following steps to meet the requirements of your customers, the lending institutions, and the agencies that insure loans for housing. Take these steps before you buy the land.

Step One

Go through the entire cautionary procedure that we have already outlined regarding the investigating of the land for undesirable characteristics. Check with local planning boards concerning the possibility that a heavy industrial enterprise will be built adjacent to your sites in the future; and check with local, state, and federal highway departments concerning the construction of new highways through the area, which could result in future condemnation proceedings. If septic systems are to be used, ask the county engineer to make soil percolation tests to determine the absorption characteristics of the soil. Investigate the availability of water, gas, electricity, and other utilities. If wells are to be used, get as much information as possible about the adequacy of the underground water supply. Know in the early stages of planning whether water will be supplied by individual wells or by a community well. If water is to be available from a local utilities company, talk to officers of this company about the adequacy of the supply. Find out if the area is susceptible to flooding.

See whether city, county, or rural fire protection will be available to residents and how such protection—or lack of it—will affect fire insurance rates for residences. Investigate the landscaping potential of the soil. Will topsoil have to be hauled in for lawns and shrubs, or is there sufficient topsoil for landscaping purposes? The ultimate disposition of the existing topsoil of the area will depend heavily upon the topography and the methods used to clear and level the land. Find out if access to public transportation, schools, and churches will be difficult for the anticipated residents of the area. Will certain natural features, such as nearby mountains or prevailing winds, cause undesirable localized climatic conditions that might hinder sales of the completed houses? (A high ridge directly to the south, for example, will shade the area from the winter sun.)

Step Two

Investigate all building and zoning codes applicable to the area. Areas that fall within the jurisdiction of a county often have different building codes from those within the jurisdiction of a city. Generally speaking, even if building codes aren't particularly stringent, they are rigidly enforced.

Step Three

Discuss your project with a local surveyor, an architect, the county engineer, and the county planning commission. Make up preliminary sketches to illustrate the potential development of the sites. Include in the sketch the number of sites to be developed, the types of houses to be built, the cost estimates for site development, preliminary time schedules, and other pertinent information.

Step Four

Ask the Federal Housing Administration for a preliminary analysis of the tract. This FHA service, which is free, is designed to aid in the development of site locations and land planning.

These steps should be taken before you buy the land. At this point, if you plan to use FHA mortgage insurance, you should talk with an FHA representative before committing yourself to buy the land.

DEVELOPING THE PLANS

By the time you have branched out into land development, you will know that the quality of the sites that you develop is about as important as the quality of the houses that you build. Since land planning is a specialized field, you will need the services of architects, land surveyors, and engineers to prepare land plats. These professionals can help you with the following:

1. Preparing topographic and land-use surveys, which show contour lines and the locations of streams, woods, roads, rock outcroppings, and other natural land features that will affect planning.
2. Compiling a list of deed restrictions, protective covenants, zoning ordinances, and other regulations enforced by local agencies, which will affect the legal status of the tract deed.
3. Working up a preliminary layout of the lots, streets, sidewalks, and possibly alleys and other features.
4. Showing access areas to such utilities as water and sewers.

Before you proceed any further, you should contact the FHA to schedule the balance of the work in preparing the detailed development plan that will show lot lines and street lines as well as the finished grade elevations. When all of this is done, you may complete a plat of the tract for filing. Finally, file the plat and restrictions with the appropriate local agency or land office. When this is complete, you are ready to plan construction of the houses.

THE ROLE OF THE FHA

While the FHA does no planning or design work itself, it does offer many services to builders and prospective homeowners. The primary role of the FHA is to improve the quality of development programs and land planning. To this end it has established standards for subdivisions and street improvements, which will upgrade the livability of an area and assure a more lasting value for the homeowner. As these higher standards are adopted and put into use, the long-term loans that the FHA insures will be provided with a more effective guarantee. And even if you don't plan to sell your houses under FHA-insured loans, you will find the FHA services of value.

By enhancing the ability of the prospective homeowners to obtain loans elsewhere, the services of the FHA work not only to the benefit of the homeowner but also to the advantage of the builder. Thus, whether the customer seeks an FHA-insured loan or one secured in some other manner, meeting FHA standards makes it easier to get financing; and when financing is relatively easy to get, you, the builder, can sell more houses with less sales effort and expense.

THE SUBDIVISION

Whether you build houses in small or large groups on a tract, the points that we have covered should be of help to you. If, however, you build as many as twenty-five or thirty houses on a tract, you are in effect developing a small community. In such a case the problems of development become more complex. Those problems are discussed in the next chapter.

12

Planning a Subdivision

When you combine subdivision development with speculative building, you are venturing into an area that requires a large amount of capital and entails many risks. By following a few rules, however, you can eliminate some of the risk elements.

With the professional help that we have talked about in the previous chapter, you can handle the technical aspects of land development. But in subdivision planning, you must also know how to develop an environment that will appeal to the buying public. This means, in essence, that while a tract of land may be suitable for building, it may be virtually worthless as a subdivision. For example, it may be far from traveled routes or located next to some objectionable area. Therefore, the major factor in successful planning and developing is being able to combine the natural attributes of the land that is available with a technically created environment that will be pleasing to the most people.

The more you know about land, and about the technical and economic problems of developing it—and about the tastes of the buying public—the more perceptive you will be in seeing both *building* and *selling* opportunities in certain tracts. With such knowledge, you should avoid making costly mistakes.

CREATING A LIFE-STYLE FOR THE HOMEOWNER

What people want in housing depends to some extent upon their income or their self-defined social status. The established housing trends of the region also play a role, and of course trends can change from time to time and from one place to another. But the cardinal rule is: *People don't just buy houses, they buy a life-style.* Paradoxically, despite their professed need to "get away from it all," people still tend to congregate in neighborhoods, close to the amenities of civilization, such as neighborhood stores, suburban shopping centers, schools, churches, parks, and so forth. These are the amenities needed for family living.

Some subdivision planners include in their plans some facilities, such as a playground or a small store. If you can't do this, try to locate your subdivision as close to existing facilities as possible. Perhaps after your subdivision is built, entrepreneurs will build some businesses (if zoning ordinances permit). If you can assure people that parks and shopping and possibly a school will be in operation by the time they start moving into the new houses, you will greatly influence the sales of the houses. If such assurances aren't forthcoming, you may have chosen the wrong location for your subdivision.

The Accessibility of Schools and Churches

If you have chosen to build your subdivision in a relatively sparsely settled area, the chances are that there are no schools nearby. This might be a deterrent in attracting families with children, particularly children of elementary school age. Yet, when all factors are considered, the best choice in land that is available to you might be in such an area. In that case, you should investigate to see if land is available upon which an elementary school might be built later. You might even be able to set aside land in your tract for a school and either give it or sell it at cost to the school board. Many people believe churches create a more stable community, and having them near your subdivision can make it more attractive.

Suburban Shopping Centers

Many suburban dwellers say that they don't like to live jammed up against a shopping center. They do, however, appreciate the availability of one within driving distance of a mile or so. If there are no shopping centers within a short drive of your proposed subdivision, there is the possibility that one is in the planning stage. This is more likely to be the case in an area where other builders and developers are active.

Recreation

One of the strongest motivating factors in the exodus from the cities to the suburbs is that people want room for their children to play. Also, many people associate the additional space that they hope to get in suburban living with a "country atmosphere." The ideal environment that they hope for (but don't always get) is an area where many of the existing trees have been left in their natural settings and there is a playground nearby for children of the subteen ages. To the average suburban homeowner, the nearby playground means safety and security for their children, and it is a powerful selling point for houses in a suburban subdivision.

Some developers have even gone so far as to include a playground in the subdivision, sometimes in the center of the area with the houses built around its perimeter. This gives easy access to all the houses in the subdivision, and in some cases the playground equipment is actually in range of the parents' vision.

A swimming pool or community recreation center will also offer an inducement to prospective buyers. One developer actually donated land for a swimming pool, then assisted the homeowners in arranging financing for a nonprofit corporation to maintain the pool. When the construction of the pool and the organization of the project were complete, the developer turned the facility over to the homeowners. This worked to his own benefit as well as to the homeowners', since the pool attracted other buyers to the subdivision.

Transportation—Public and Private

When you calculate the accessibility of a proposed subdivision to areas where most of the residents will be employed, the most important factor to consider is not distance but commuting time. Most people don't like to spend more than a half-hour traveling to and from work. When this is interpreted in miles, the factors of rush-hour congestion have to be considered. You will also have to consider the quality and accessibility of the roads that connect your subdivision with main routes. Also to be considered in locating the subdivision is its accessibility to public transportation; a rapid-transit line could change the commuters' problems dramatically.

Another possibility is locating the subdivision near the major industry of the area, which virtually puts the suburban dweller on top of his or her work. Many people like this arrangement. And, of course, in such a case the nature of the major industry will determine the average income level of the residents, which will, in turn, determine the kinds of houses that will be in demand.

LAND-USE REGULATIONS AND THEIR PURPOSE

Generally speaking, local and regional laws spell out the ways in which land can be used, and local and regional planning boards administer these regulations. For example, the regulations may stipulate that the land in certain areas is to be used solely for residential dwellings, while other areas are set aside for industrial developments. In certain areas, federal or state governing bodies dictate the kinds of structures that can be placed in view of the shorelines of major waterways.

The purpose of land-use planning is to bring order into what the governing bodies believe would otherwise be chaos, to keep the shorelines and countryside attractive, and to put the available natural resources to the best possible use. In general, land-use planning protects the property owner by regulating the kinds of developments that can be built adjacent to each other. The precautions that you should take concerning land use are twofold: (1) you must check existing land-use regulations to be certain that the development you are planning will be permitted in the area, and (2) if there are no land-use regulations in existence in the area where you plan to develop, you should seek some means of protecting your own investment; you may do this by building adjacent to a similar development or by acquiring some surrounding land.

EVALUATING THE NATURAL FEATURES OF THE TRACT

The first question to ask yourself in evaluating a tract of land is, Can this land be developed in such a manner as to attract customers? The second question to ask is, Will the topography and other physical features of the land allow a profitable development? Among the physical features that you will examine are the size of the tract and the soil conditions.

The Size of the Tract

As a rule of thumb, you can assume that the larger a tract is, the more flexibility you will have in developing it. However, size advantages must be weighed against such features as drainage and vulnerability to flooding. Everything else being equal, a larger tract will be less costly to develop, on a per-lot basis, than a smaller tract. Size also offers a certain amount of freedom, and if the development is properly laid out, there will be some protection from encroachments by undesirable developments.

A method that small builders often use to assure the environmental quality of an area is to buy blocks of lots from large-scale developers, who in turn guarantee that houses built on adjacent areas will be of a price range and quality comparable to those of their own development. Or several builders may join together to buy a large tract. Several West Coast builders did this, and then formed a corporation to secure necessary financing for a large development.

Topography of the Land

Is the land level, gradually sloping, steeply sloping, or hilly? Don't take it for granted that level land will offer the fewest development problems; some areas of level land have sour soil, and underground water surfaces during the wet season. Such conditions would necessitate the laying of an expensive drainage system and create problems in the drainage of septic systems as well.

Generally speaking, land that lies in a uniform, slight grade should present the fewest problems in developing, although careful planning will still be necessary in the siting of the lots, to be sure that the lots on the lower levels are not catch-basins for the accumulated drainage of the higher levels of the tract.

Land that is steeply sloping can present special problems in drainage and may require retaining walls between the various lots. Also, expert workmanship is necessary in the leveling of the lots to conserve the existing topsoil; for example, when successive lots are bulldozed down to grade, all the previous soil may be scraped off the upper sides of the lots, leaving an impervious or rocky soil in which neither shrubs nor grass will grow.

The first question to consider regarding hilly land is, Will this kind of development appeal to customers? Even if all factors point to customer appeal, hilly land presents some problems in development, but with careful planning it can give good results. There will be more expense in excavating and grading than on level land. The type of structure most adaptable to hilly land is the split-level house, with the recreation room or family room and garage at ground level.

Soil Conditions

The soil condition is an inherent part of the housing package that you will be preparing for your prospective customers. The average depth of the topsoil, its suitability for growing grass and shrubs, the kind of subsoil, the outcroppings of rock, the slope of the land—all are factors to consider regarding soil. A thorough understanding of the soil conditions will result in more attractive and livable housing sites.

Sour Soil.   In one instance a builder built houses on a level but poorly drained area. When some of his houses were occupied, the word began to travel around that starting lawns and shrubs there required considerable trouble and expensive preparation of the soil, because poor drainage caused a sour condition of the soil. The builder could not be forced to remedy this condition; however, a decline in sales ultimately forced him out of speculative building.

Accumulated Ground Water

In still another case, a septic drainage system that was laid in a heavy clay subsoil resulted in the surfacing of septic water in the yards of new homeowners. Customer complaint followed complaint, and when first the builder and then county officials refused to take action, a few complaints were formally filed with the state. State officials determined that the responsibility for correcting the situation rested with the new homeowners. Slowly, through a procession of new owners who were gulled into buying the houses by the previous owners, the situation is being corrected, and there is a promise that a sewer line will be brought into the area in the future. Meanwhile, the builder has switched from building houses to selling cut-rate building materials.

The above problems could have been avoided if the builders had applied even a rudimentary knowledge of the soil requirements for livable building sites. In both cases, they developed the land because it was cheap. When difficulties arose, they felt that they were not financially able to make the necessary corrections, and they accepted the legal loophole that was offered. But as a result, the buying public forced both these builders out of the business.

STORM DRAINAGE

Builders who are in too much of a hurry to analyze lot conditions and make plans accordingly have made some remarkable blunders in the siting of houses. For example, one Oregon builder sited a house in a swale that must for centuries have been the catch-basin for the storm runoff from the hillside above. He did this through a combination of miscalculations and negligence. First, he examined the site in the dry season and determined that the level terrain of the swale basin would be suitable for a house. Second, he subcontracted the entire construction of the house to two carpenters, leaving them unsupervised as they worked on the house well into the rainy season. Third, by early the following summer, when the house was ready for occupancy, the swale basin was beginning to dry and presented an acceptable appearance. Finally, by the following spring, after repeated complaints from the new owners of the house, the builder was forced to install a difficult and expensive drainage system to divert the storm runoff around the site.

PLANNING FOR UTILITIES

Before committing yourself to purchase any land, you will have to make sure that the utility companies will bring their services to a distance accessible to the sites.

Water

Many—but not all—suburban developments depend upon wells for water. Since it is difficult to induce prospective customers to buy homes in an area where they would incur the expense of drilling a well (and since the customer expects a complete housing package), you the builder will usually include either individual wells or a community well as part of the housing package. And, of course, if water from a public utility company is available in adequate supply, it will be your preferred choice. From the utility company, you will have to get the following information.
1. The date when water mains will be made accessible to the tract.
2. The fee (if any) for installing mains.

3. The fee (if any) for connecting individual lines to the main.
4. The amount of water that will be available through the mains.
5. The rate at which the customers will be charged for water consumption.

Fuel

The primary fuel used for space heating, water heating, and cooking may be natural gas, "bottled gas," fuel oil, or electricity. Your decision on which to use will depend on the availability of the various fuels, their comparative popularity with homeowners, and their prices. The kind of fuel you decide on will determine the kinds of major appliances that you will install. The choice of fuel, as it relates to convenience, price, future availability, and maintenance problems for the customer, will influence the salability of the houses. This is a particularly important decision in a time when fuels are diminishing in supply and increasing in price.

Electricity

To the average homeowner, electricity is taken for granted. When you instruct your electrical subcontractor about the specifications for installing the wiring in the homes that you build, you cannot take it for granted. For example, if the homes are to be heated electrically or many major appliances of heavy current ratings are to be a part of the housing package, the proper kind of electrical service with wiring of sufficient current-carrying capacity will have to be installed. In many areas, this service must be installed, not only in accordance with the rules of the company supplying the electricity, but also in conformity with local or state building codes. To meet all these requirements, you will have to work in close cooperation with the electric company from the outset.

Sewage

In previous sections, I touched upon septic systems as one method of sewage disposal. But your problems concerning sewage disposal will be somewhat different if you can hook up to a public sewage-disposal system. As in electrical wiring, the kinds and diameters of sewage pipe that can be used for the individual hookups will be dictated by local and state building codes. And again, you must work in cooperation with the utility company in seeing that all the requirements are met.

Streets

Through the influence of the FHA, the requirements for street improvements have become fairly standardized throughout the United States. However, standards may vary from locality to locality due to soil characteristics or other special conditions. You can get a description of these standards from your local FHA insuring office. You should also check with local highway departments concerning your plans for street improvements.

POINTS TO THINK ABOUT IN GOOD SUBDIVISION PLANNING

Two basic rules for good subdivision planning are:

Make yourself aware of the advantages and disadvantages of the particular land tract that you are considering. This means don't jump to conclusions. Just because the land is located in a certain area, don't take it for granted that it has desirable and/or undesirable characteristics similar to those of adjacent tracts. Local geological variations, for example, can mean variations in soil or drainage conditions. Ask questions. If the tract has been avoided by other developers, or if it is offered for sale more cheaply than adjacent tracts, there may be a reason.

Know exactly what is an advantage and what is a disadvantage in land development. Consider such factors as local climatic conditions, the property tax base of the county in which the land is located, and the trends of the buying public.

Work out a plan for solving the usual and special problems presented by this land tract. Then analyze the problems in terms of cost. By this time you will have familiarized yourself with the optimum relationship between the cost of developing land and the sales price of the houses you intend to build.

The following suggestions should help you in the

creation of a final package that will have customer appeal.

1. As much as possible, work with the natural environment of the area rather than using expensive methods of altering the environment. This means leaving as many of the healthy existing trees in their natural setting as possible and retaining such natural features as rock outcroppings whenever feasible.

2. If the tract is large, divide it into several distinct areas. This helps to bring segments of the tract to completion faster and alleviates the monotony that might creep into the design of a large tract.

3. Relate your development plans to those of the region, if such plans have been made.

4. Incorporate as many safety features as possible into the design of the subdivision. For example, when working out play areas and routes to schools and stores, avoid built-in traffic hazards for children.

5. When planning garages and parking areas, relate them to the rest of the area so as to minimize noise and maximize the beauty and atmosphere of the total tract.

6. Leave space for the residents to breathe, play, and live. Include small parks and play areas in this space. Think also of the future, when even more space might be needed for a restful and relaxed way of life for your suburban dwellers.

7. If possible, work with utility companies to lay telephone and electric lines underground. This requires especially careful planning to keep them

out of the path of any future excavations that might be made to install water or sewer lines.

By now you may well say, "But not all builders go to this much trouble to develop subdivisions." While it is true that in the heights of the building booms that followed World War II, the Korean conflict, and the Vietnam War, many construction companies built as quickly and cheaply as they could, it is also true that by now most of these builders have either improved their methods or gotten out of the building business. Their places have been taken by a breed of builders who study the markets, learn new and better building methods, analyze the relationship between construction costs and selling prices, and work to create a total housing package of the best possible quality for its price. These are the builders who stay in business year after year. They are the builders with whom you will be competing.

INDEX

207